INFANTRY RIFLEMAN

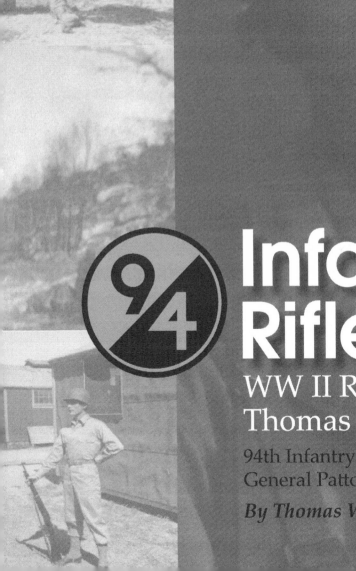

94 Infantry Rifleman

WW II Reflections of Thomas W. Smith

94th Infantry Division,
General Patton's Third Army

By Thomas W. Smith, III

ACKNOWLEDGEMENTS

This book was written by the family of Thomas Warner Smith (TW). While TW's oldest son Tommy was the lead author, he considers his role to be more of an editor, recognizing the significant work and contributions of his brothers, sisters and mother. Tommy and his brother Jefferson spent many dozens of hours tracking down and ensuring the accuracy of the details of the stories captured in this book, including interviews with TW's friends and colleagues. The two brothers also spent untold hours discussing the book's format and structure, taking and reviewing photographs and verifying sources. Many of the stories also were contributed by TW's three other children, Janene, Randy and Jennifer, and by TW's wife Janet. Having followed in his father's footsteps in attending the Citadel, Randy contributed many stories that he and his friends heard from TW and his fellow veterans over the years, all of which added greatly to this book. TW's oldest child Janene contributed critical photographs and many stories learned from direct accounts from TW and his friends. TW's daughter Jennifer contributed editing and feedback, while TW's wife Janet coordinated historical materials, verified facts and details, and helped track down sources. In deference to the sacrifice of TW and his fellow GIs, many of whom sacrificed their lives during WW II, the family took great pains to ensure the accuracy of these accounts, and to avoid exaggeration or embellishment. Collectively, TW's family worked on this book to preserve a small piece of Smith family history for future generations. The following is brief background on TW's wife and children.

Janet Meyer Smith (nee Janet Marie Meyer). TW's wife Janet was born in Melrose, Minnesota. She was the fourth of eight children, born just minutes before her twin brother Jack. Janet attended the College of St. Theresa and graduated from the Minnesota School of Business before moving to Washington, D.C. in 1952. She was working for the Automotive Safety Foundation when she met TW. They were married on February 17, 1962. Janet later worked for the Allstate Foundation before raising five children fulltime. She has served as a local election officer and as a volunteer with the American Red Cross, the Historic Alexandria Docents, and St. Anthony's PTA. She is a member of Emily King's Old Dominion Doll Club and the Northern Virginia Antique Arts Association. She also enjoys volunteering with a local retirement community.

Janene Smith Mitchell (nee Janet Allene Smith). Named after her mother and paternal grandmother, Janene was born on January 20, 1963 at George Washington Hospital in Washington, D.C. She received a Bachelor of Science degree in Commerce with a concentration in Accounting from the McIntire School of Commerce, University of Virginia. She is a Certified Public Accountant and after 17 years with PriceWaterhouseCoopers now works for the Reznick Group. She has been an active volunteer with the Junior League of Washington, Historic Alexandria Docents and Blessed Sacrament School and Church. She lives in Chevy Chase, Maryland, with her husband Thomas Wilfried Mitchell and their four children, Colin Thomas, Curtis Glenn, Eric Howard and Eleanor Sylvia.

Thomas Warner Smith, III (Tommy). Tommy was born on June 27, 1964 at George Washington Hospital in Washington, D.C. Tommy graduated from the University of Virginia in 1986 with a Bachelor of Science degree and earned a Master of Engineering degree in 1987, both in civil engineering. He received his law degree from Washington & Lee University in 1990. Tommy works for the American Society of Civil Engineers as Deputy Executive Director and General Counsel and serves on the Fairfax County Board of Zoning Appeals. Tommy lives in Vienna, Virginia with his wife Marcia Mayo Smith, and their three children Grayson Thomas, Connor Joseph and Garrett Patrick.

Randolph Lee Smith (Randy). Born on August 16, 1966 in Fairfax, Virginia, Randy's middle name was in honor of Confederate General Robert E. Lee. Randy graduated from the Citadel in 1988 with a Bachelor of Science degree in Business Administration and works as a sales director at Sungard Availability Services. Randy resides in Gainesville, Virginia, where he is active with motorcycle clubs, hunting, shooting and other outdoor activities. He is married to Elizabeth Anne Smith, and they have two children, Callie Rebecca and Madeline Marie.

Jennifer Ellen Smith. Jennifer was born on August 2, 1969 in Fairfax, Virginia. She was named after her maternal grandmother, Eleanor Meyer, who passed away in 2004 at 106 years of age. Jennifer graduated with a Bachelor of Science degree in Sociology from High Point University in 1992 and works as an executive assistant at the MITRE Corporation. She enjoys volunteering with the Junior League of Northern Virginia and resides in Falls Church, Virginia.

Jefferson Thompson Smith. Born on December 8, 1970 in Fairfax, Virginia, Jefferson received his middle name after his paternal grandmother, Ossie Allene Thompson. Jefferson graduated with a business degree from the College of William and Mary in 1992 and earned an MBA from the George Washington University in 2004, and his Associate in Risk Management in 2011. He works as Assistant Director of Risk Management at the George Washington University. He is also a performer who has played a variety of roles in film, television, and commercials, including parts on the Discovery, National

Geographic, and History Channels, as well as videos for the FBI Academy and the U.S. Army. Jefferson resides in Falls Church, Virginia.

Thanks are extended to Brian Baick, David Bell, Patricia Bell, Bob Bowden, Stefan Jaeger, Ann Meyer, David Meyer, Carlo Salzano, and Marcia Smith, who also contributed stories, research or editing for this book.

Front row (left to right): Jennifer, Janet, TW and Janene; back row (left to right): Jefferson, Tommy and Randy (2010)

This book is dedicated to the WW II veterans of the 94th Infantry Division.

CONTENTS

FORWARD

The following reflects stories that we, the children of Thomas Warner Smith (TW), have heard over the years and more recently during a series of interviews. While TW did not keep a diary during the war, noting that he was *"too concerned with staying alive,"* this book includes recollections obtained from TW's files and letters, as well as World War II (WW II) books and articles that TW accumulated over the past sixty years. Epitomizing TW's deep love of history, and particularly military history, most of the material used in this book was obtained from TW's office. Direct quotes from TW's interviews or letters are in *italics*. The stories illustrate the perspective of a WW II American soldier, an infantry rifleman, who volunteered to serve his country as a private, landing in Normandy and fighting on the front lines of the Western Front at a critical point in our nation's history. Recognizing the continuity of human history and, as noted by President Harry S. Truman, that "the only new thing in the world is the history you don't know," TW's children ultimately decided to sit down with their father to ascertain the details of his military service and related activities and to document them for future generations of the Smith family.

The staggering statistic that over 50 million people were killed during the Second World War, including more than fifty countries fighting across six continents and all the world's oceans, reminds us of the significance of this single event in the history of humankind. Americans of the WW II era are often referred to as the Greatest Generation. More than 400,000 Americans were killed, including many of our father's neighbors, friends and classmates, whom he notes with dismay *"never made it back."* Many of those who survived witnessed horrific atrocities, but also unthinkable acts of courage that ultimately secured victory for the Allied Forces. Their sacrifice propelled the United States to new heights as a global super power and had a lasting impact on the world.

Our thanks to our father, who made great sacrifices to ensure the freedom that we and our children enjoy today, and to the many other heroes of WW II who gave everything they had for their country.

Janene Smith Mitchell
Thomas Warner Smith, III
Randolph Lee Smith
Jennifer Ellen Smith
Jefferson Thompson Smith

1. MILITARY ANCESTRY

Fortiter-in-re
(Gently in Manner
Strongly in Deed)

In-Lumini-Luci
(I may shine in
the light)

"Though my father seldom talked about it, I have always taken great
pride in his service to his country in WW I."

Thomas Warner Smith (TW) was born on July 12, 1923, in Washington, D.C., and was the only child of Thomas Smith Senior (Tom Sr.) and Allene Thompson Smith (nee Ossie Allene Thompson). Soon after his birth, the country was entering a depression and oppressive events were occurring overseas that would later lead to another world war. Unfortunately, war is a consistent theme throughout the recorded history of human civilization, and TW and his ancestors participated in a number of historic wars involving the United States. TW's family history of military service dates at least as far back as the Revolutionary War and includes soldiers in his maternal and paternal ancestry, some of whom are depicted in the T.W. Smith military ancestry tree on the following page.

Each of these wars was critical to preserving the democracy and freedom we enjoy in the United States today and each of these wars exacted a heavy toll, with thousands of American lives sacrificed for their country. According to Department of Defense records compiled for a 2009 Congressional Research Service report, these wars resulted in the following American casualties:[1]

---

1   American deaths in subsequent wars have included 36,574 in the Korean War (1950-1953), 58,220 in the Vietnam War (1964-1973), 382 in the Persian Gulf War (1990-1991), 1,371 in Afghanistan (as of November 7, 2010) and 4,427 in Iraq (as of November 7, 2010).

T.W. Smith Military Ancestry

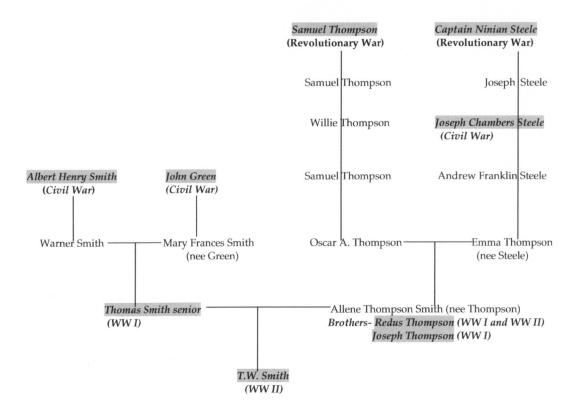

U.S. Wartime Casualties

War	Number Serving	Dead	Wounded
Revolutionary War (1775-1783)	Unknown	4,435	6,188
Civil War (1861-1865)	2,213,363	500,000+ (364,451 Union; est. 162,000 Confederate)	281,881 (Union)
WW I (1917-1918)	4,734,991	116,516	204,002
WW II (1941-1945)	16,112,560	405,399	670,846

As noted, the Civil War resulted in more American fatalities than any other war fought by the United States to date, due largely to the fact that Americans were fighting and killing fellow Americans. The devastation of the Civil War is even worse considering the percentage of the U.S. population lost at that time. WW II, however, was the first American war resulting in more American battle deaths than non-battle deaths, including deaths from disease, infection or accidents.

While most of TW's ancestors survived these momentous wars, not all of them were so fortunate. Below is a summary of their military service.

Revolutionary War

In 1769, George Washington wrote George Mason noting:

> At a time, when our lordly masters in Great Britain will be satisfied with nothing less than the deprivation of American freedom, it seems highly necessary that something should be done to avert the stroke, and maintain the liberty, which we have derived from our ancestors. . . .That no man should scruple, or hesitate a moment, to use arms in defence of so valuable a blessing, on which all the good and evil of life depends, is clearly my opinion.

Six years later, America was engaged in a long battle for freedom from Great Britain in the face of overwhelming odds, and Washington knew full well that "the fate of unborn millions will now depend, under God, on the courage and conduct of this army." Although concerned about the dire circumstances of "my situation and that of this army," and lamenting in 1776 that "few people know the predicament we are in," George Washington was motivated by "the goodness of our cause" and his observation that "perseverance and spirit have done wonders in all ages."

One of TW's ancestors who fought for the goodness of America's cause was Captain Ninian Steele. Buried in Statesville, North Carolina, Captain Steele lived from 1738 to 1813 and was TW's great-great-great-great grandfather. The Steele family traces its history back to Ireland and Scotland, and includes bloodlines to TW through TW's maternal grandmother named Emma Jackson Thompson, nee Steele. In a family history of the Steele family published in 1901, the author, Dr. Newton Steele, who was Captain Steele's great grandson, described Captain Steele as a patriot soldier and relayed an account of Revolutionary War times from a letter he possessed from an eighty year old woman whose mother was an orphan raised in Captain Steele's home:

> This lady says that she has heard her mother say that Ninian Steele was a soldier in the war, and she used to hear her tell how afraid the wife and children of Ninian Steele sometimes were, while he was gone to the war, and the British and Tory

troops were reported to be in the community. There was no man at home to protect them, and the terror of those terrible days and the nights of suspense deeply impressed their minds with the facts and the reasons for them.

Providing insight into the Steeles' sentiments of war and peace, Dr. Steele described Captain Ninian Steele as follows:

> Ninian Steele was known in his county as a "peacemaker." Tradition has it that he sometimes actually paid the amount of money in dispute between neighbors in order to stop a neighborhood broil. While he did not hesitate, as we believe, to act the soldier in war, he was emphatically a man of peace in times of peace. This was certainly an excellent trait of character—a noble heritage to leave his children.

TW's maternal grandfather was named Oscar Adolphus Thompson. The Thompson family traces its history back to its immigration to the United States from Lancaster, England, in the late 1500's. A family history of the Thompson Family written in 1905 notes that 28 Thompson family members fought in the Revolutionary War, including Samuel Thompson, who we believe was TW's great-great-great-great grandfather. The family history further notes that Samuel Thompson enlisted with Lee's Legions Armand Corps and served at Valley Forge in 1778. Samuel Thompson was wounded at King's Mountain in 1780 and was honorably discharged in April 1783, the same month that Congress ratified a preliminary peace treaty with Great Britain.

With the loss of some 25,000 Americans, or about one percent of the population, the Revolutionary War was put in perspective by General Washington's early observation that "no danger is to be considered when put in competition with the magnitude of the cause." TW has always appreciated the magnitude of the cause and has been known to fly two American flags at his house. Each year, he goes to great lengths to celebrate our nation's independence on the Fourth of July, with what President John Adams aptly predicted would include "pomp and parade, with shows, games, sports, guns, bells, bonfires, and illuminations, from one end of this continent to the other, from this time forward forever more."[2]

Civil War

Eighty years following its independence, the U.S. was involved in an internal war where it was common to find brothers and cousins fighting against each other. Following decades of disagreements over issues including tariffs, slavery and states' rights,

---

2 John Adams was incorrect only in his prediction that the celebration would be held on July 2nd, the date of the initial vote of independence.

the Union Army of the North and the Confederate Army of the South fought each other for four long and arduous years in the Civil War, or as TW and his Southern ancestors call it, the War Between the States. In his Second Inaugural Address in March 1865, just one month before he was assassinated, President Lincoln explained that:

> Neither party expected for the war, the magnitude, or the duration, which it has already attained…Both read the same Bible, and pray to the same God; and each invokes His aid against the other. It may seem strange that any men should dare to ask a just God's assistance in wringing their bread from the sweat of other men's faces; but let us judge not, that we be not judged. The prayers of both could not be answered; that of neither has been answered fully. The Almighty has His own purposes.

Referring again to TW's maternal grandmother's ancestry, Dr. Newton Steele also wrote of the Steele family's participation in the Civil War:

> During the great Civil War between the Southern and Northern States, 1861-65, twenty-four descendants of Ninian Steele were soldiers in the Confederate army, and so far as I know, not one in the army of the North. All of them lived in the South. There were fourteen Confederate soldiers who before or since that war, were directly connected with the Steele family by marriage.

Among the twenty-four Steele descendants in the Civil war was Joseph Chambers Steele, TW's great-great grandfather. Joseph Steele volunteered in October 1861 to serve in the 17th Regiment Arkansas Infantry. He was captured at the siege of Vicksburg and was released in a prisoner exchange. Joseph was captured again during General Sterling Price's last raid into Missouri in the fall of 1864 and later escaped. He finally surrendered at Jackson Port, Arkansas, in June 1865, almost two months after General Robert E. Lee's surrender at Appomattox.[3]

On his father's side, TW had two great-grandfathers who fought in the Civil War. Albert Henry Smith was born in 1833 and was TW's great-grandfather on his paternal grandfather's side. Albert Henry was a farmer and a teacher in a one-room school house in rural Alabama. His son Warner, who was TW's grandfather, relayed to TW his memory of sitting on his front porch at five years of age watching his father leave for the war, walking with fourteen other new soldiers to Jacksonville, Alabama where they boarded a train to Virginia. Albert Henry served in Company E of the 48th Alabama Regiment, Confederate Army under the leadership of Major General Evander McIvor Law. Law was an

---

3 Additionally, Dr. Steele notes that two descendants of Captain Ninian Steele were soldiers in the Spanish-American War of 1898. Describing the low family participation in the Spanish-American War, Dr. Steele notes that "there were no real 'defend the flag' or 'fight for your firesides' arguments to stir the people to war."

1856 graduate of the Citadel, the military college of South Carolina where TW would go to college eighty-five years later.

After being wounded in two prior battles, Albert Henry Smith was mortally wounded during the Second Battle of Manassas in late 1862. Confederate records dated January 16, 1863, include A.H. Smith on the list of "killed and wounded in Taliaferro's Brigade,

Confederate records of Albert Henry Smith, including from left to right (i) muster role identifying A.H. Smith as present on April 12, 1862, with the 48th Alabama Regiment, (ii) register indicating A.H. Smith of Company E., 48th Regiment died on November 24, 1862, and (iii) Confederate record including A.H. Smith on list of killed and wounded in Taliaferro's Brigade.

Albert Henry Smith

from the time General Lee took command at Gordonsville, until the Army left the Valley." William Booth Taliaferro, whose brigade was under the command of Major General Thomas J. "Stonewall" Jackson, was also seriously wounded during the Second Battle of Manassas.

Following news of Albert Henry's death, his wife Elizabeth wrote a letter dated January 30, 1863, to Confederate Sergeant J.B. Smole. She sought the return of the $96 Albert Henry left when he died, further stating "can't you get Mr. Smith's clothes also or do as you think best about them, very respectfully, your friend, Elizabeth Smith."

That same year, recognizing the heavy casualties of the Civil War, President Lincoln declared in his November 1863 Gettysburg Address that:

> We here highly resolve that these dead shall not have died in vain; that this nation, under God, shall have a new birth of freedom; and that this government of the people, by the people, for the people, shall not perish from the earth.

Soon after Albert Henry Smith's death, John Green entered the Confederate service on February 13, 1863, as Captain of Company L, 7th Alabama Calvary. John Green was TW's great-grandfather on his paternal grandmother's side, and he was also a farmer from rural Alabama. John Green was wounded in the Battle of Unionville, Tennessee, and later received a pension from the state of Alabama for his Confederate service before passing away on October 8, 1902. TW's father, Tom Sr., personally recalled his grandfather John Green and heard him and other former members of the 7th Alabama Calvary discuss their Civil War exploits. Visiting Alabama often during his childhood, TW heard his father speak many times with friends and family in Alabama of their Civil War ancestors.

The Confederate Army surrendered at Appomattox on April 9, 1865, after which a General Order in 1868 designated May 30th "for the purpose of strewing with flowers, or otherwise decorating the graves of comrades who died in defense of their country during the late rebellion, and whose bodies now lie in almost every city, village, and hamlet churchyard in the land." The service was first held at Arlington Cemetery, which was created by the Union Army during the Civil War on property then owned by General Robert E. Lee's family. The property was confiscated by the Union Army for use as a hospital and burial ground following the Lee family's departure during the war. Arlington Cemetery now has over 300,000 graves, including veterans from all the nation's wars. This service, formerly known as Decoration Day, became known as Memorial Day and continues to be recognized on the last Monday in May in honor of those who died in service to their country.

Some argue that Memorial Day had its roots in earlier Decoration Day gatherings held in the South. In any case, TW and his father grew up recognizing both Memorial Day and Decoration Day. For many years, TW drove his father and sons down to Alabama on the third Sunday in May to celebrate "Decoration Day" at the Hill cemetery near Collinsville, Alabama. Despite searches in Virginia and Alabama cemeteries, TW has been unable to locate the grave of his great-grandfather Albert Henry Smith. Although Albert Henry's grave likely remains undecorated and unmarked, TW's cousins dedicated a memorial in 2009 to Albert Henry at the Hill cemetery, not far from the Confederate soldier's homewtown.

World War I

TW's father, Tom Sr., was born in Collinsville, Alabama on February 6, 1890. Benjamin Harrison was President at the time and was actively supporting a naval expansion and the annexation of Hawaii, from which the United States was leasing Pearl Harbor as a naval base. Tom Sr. was the sixth of seven children and is pictured at five years of age next to his mother on the far right in the family picture (facing page), taken in 1895.

Tom Sr. grew up on a farm working long hours raising crops and tending farm animals. In search of a new life away from cows, corn and cotton, Tom Sr. took the Civil

Tom Sr. Family 1895

Service exam in an effort to obtain federal government employment. TW remembers his father telling of how he learned the results of his exam.

> *My Dad said he was out in the fields working as usual with a hoe. One of his brothers ran out to him with an envelope containing the results of the exam. In his excitement upon learning that he passed the exam, my Dad threw his hoe into the air in celebration of the fact that he would never have to hoe again.*

With $10 in his pocket, Tom Sr. left his hometown for Washington, D.C. in 1911. He waited to leave Alabama just ten days after first exercising his right to vote in local elections, a civic duty that Tom Sr. would dutifully exercise over the next seventy years. Upon arriving in Washington, Tom Sr. worked as a clerk. Meanwhile, his sister and five brothers continued to farm in Alabama, an occupation they would continue there for the rest of their lives.

A year after arriving in our nation's capital, Tom Sr. participated in his first Presidential election, voting for Woodrow Wilson, who narrowly defeated Theodore Roosevelt and William Howard Taft in 1912. Four years later, Tom Sr. voted again for Woodrow Wilson, who was re-elected in 1916 under the slogan "He kept us out of the war." Over the following year, however, foreign pressures increased in a worldwide conflict that would later become known as World War I.

The war started years earlier after a Serbian student assassinated the heir to the Austro-Hungarian throne in June of 1914. The assassination triggered Austria-Hungary's declaration of war on Serbia, and each side was soon joined by other countries with longstanding treaties and alliances. Although initially attempting to stay neutral, the U.S. was increasingly drawn into the conflict. In 1915 a German submarine sank the British cruise liner Lusitania, killing more than 1,100 people, including 128 Americans. Germany's policy of unrestricted submarine warfare on any ship destined for Britain, even from a neutral country, increasingly put America's interests at risk, forcing the President and Congress to join the complicated global conflict that President Wilson called "a war to end all wars." The United States declared war on Germany in April 1917 and joined Allied Powers including France, Britain and Russia. Months later, the United States declared war on Austria-Hungary, one of the Central Powers that included Germany and Turkey. During the course of the war, the Ottoman Empire and Bulgaria joined the Central Powers. Italy, Romania, Japan and China joined the Allied Powers. Eventually, the war included countries from every inhabited continent.

From the outset, President Wilson explained that "it is a fearful thing to lead this great peaceful people into war, into the most terrible and disastrous of all wars," but also that American soldiers were needed "to make the world safe for democracy." To assemble an American fighting force to make the world safe for democracy, it became necessary to institute a draft. The local draft exempted farmers, including each of Tom Sr.'s brothers, whose service producing food at home was deemed critical to a nation at war. Having left his hoe years earlier in Alabama, Tom Sr. was not subject to the farmer exemption and instead was eligible to be drafted for military service on the Western Front. Although not what he originally contemplated, Tom Sr. would indeed find a new life, replacing his hoe with a machine gun. In 1917, while his brothers and sister continued farming peacefully in Collinsville, Alabama, the twenty-seven year old Tom Sr. became one of 2.7 million American men between the ages of twenty-one and thirty-one who were drafted to fight in the "Great War" that later became known as WW I.

The United States eventually sent some two million men, often called "doughboys," to fight "over there" in the deadly and muddy trench warfare of the Western Front. In many ways, the experiences Tom Sr. had during WW I and the key players involved would later play important roles in TW's own military experience.

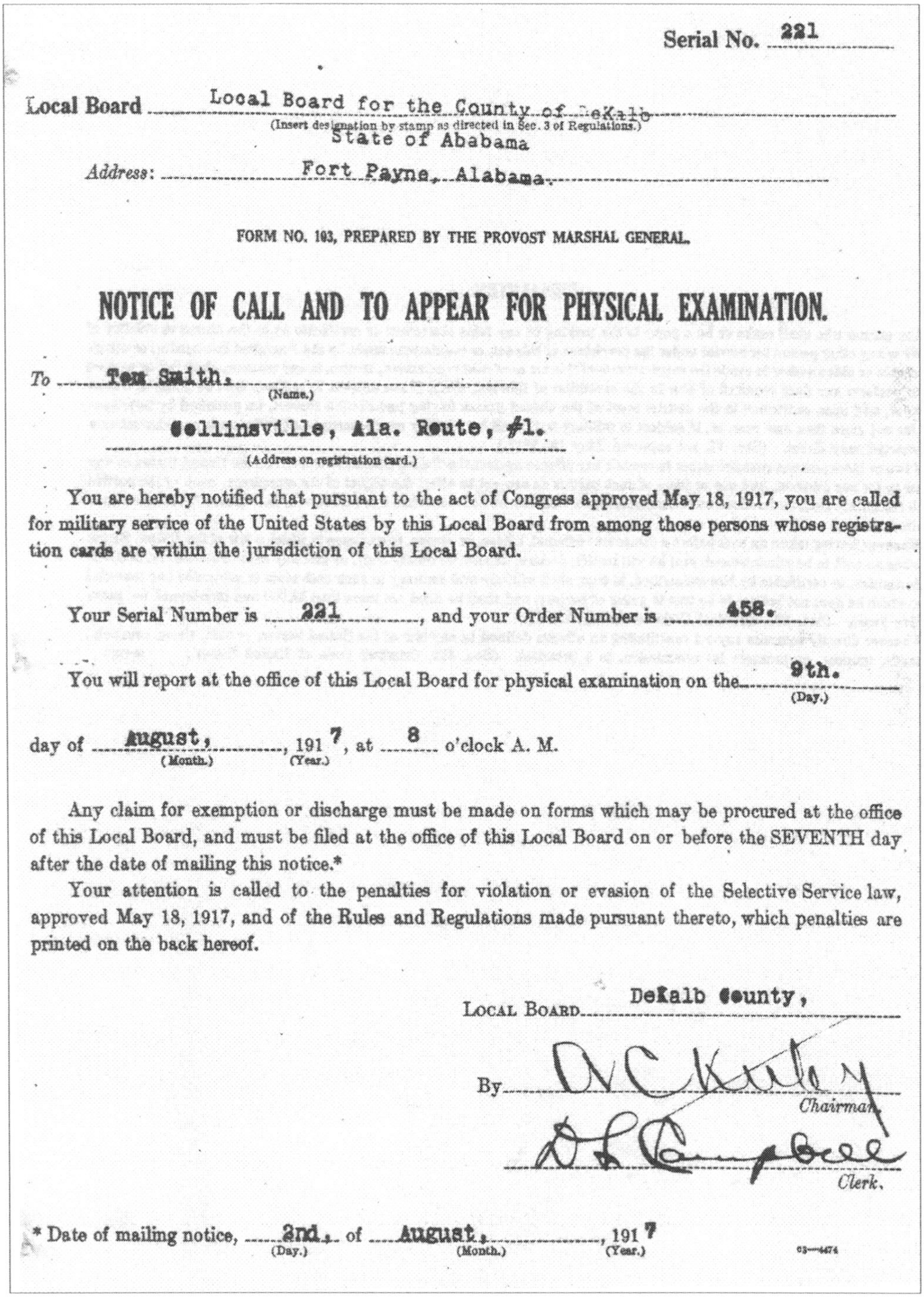

Serial No. **221**

Local Board ___Local Board for the County of DeKalb___
(Insert designation by stamp as directed in Sec. 3 of Regulations.)
State of Ababama

Address: ___Fort Payne, Alabama___

FORM NO. 103, PREPARED BY THE PROVOST MARSHAL GENERAL.

NOTICE OF CALL AND TO APPEAR FOR PHYSICAL EXAMINATION.

To ___Tom Smith,___
(Name.)

___Collinsville, Ala. Route, #1.___
(Address on registration card.)

You are hereby notified that pursuant to the act of Congress approved May 18, 1917, you are called for military service of the United States by this Local Board from among those persons whose registration cards are within the jurisdiction of this Local Board.

Your Serial Number is ___221___, and your Order Number is ___458.___

You will report at the office of this Local Board for physical examination on the ___9th.___
(Day.)

day of ___August,___ 191 **7**, at ___8___ o'clock A. M.
(Month.) (Year.)

Any claim for exemption or discharge must be made on forms which may be procured at the office of this Local Board, and must be filed at the office of this Local Board on or before the SEVENTH day after the date of mailing this notice.*

Your attention is called to the penalties for violation or evasion of the Selective Service law, approved May 18, 1917, and of the Rules and Regulations made pursuant thereto, which penalties are printed on the back hereof.

LOCAL BOARD ___DeKalb County,___

By _____
Chairman

_____
Clerk.

* Date of mailing notice, ___2nd,___ of ___August,___ 191 **7**
(Day.) (Month.) (Year.)

03—4474

Tom Sr.'s draft notice dated August 2, 1917

Tom Sr., pictured second from left

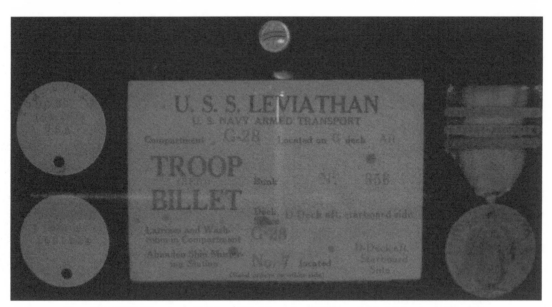

Tom Sr.'s WW I dog tags, Rainbow Division pin, WW I medal (with bars reading "St. Mihiel, Meuse-Argonne and Defensive Sector"), and Billet Slip for the U.S.S. Leviathan, his transport ship during WW I, all of which are framed and hang over TW's desk.

U.S.S. Leviathan in New York Harbor

Along with some 14,000 troops, Tom Sr. was transported to the combat zone on the U.S.S. Leviathan. Originally built in Hamberg, Germany, as a passenger liner called the S.S. Vaterland, the United States seized the German ship upon joining the war in April 1917. Aptly renamed the U.S.S. Leviathan, Tom Sr.'s transport was the largest ship in the U.S. Navy during WW I and, in fact, was the largest ship in the world until 1922.

Tom Sr. was a machine gunner in the Machine Gun Company of the 166th Ohio Regiment of the famous Rainbow Division (42nd Infantry Division). Tom Sr. served under Rainbow Division Chief of Staff Douglas MacArthur, who would later command the U.S. Army Forces in the Far East while TW fought in WW II.

TW notes with pride that his father served as a private and *"fought in France at Château Thierry, Saint Mihiel, and Meuse-Argonne."* During more than a month of brutal warfare in WW I's final campaign, known as the Meuse-Argonne offensive, Tom Sr.'s 42nd Infantry Division fought through German machine gun fire and broke out of the Argonne Forrest, reaching Sedan, France, on November 8, 1918. This bloody offensive was designed and coordinated in part by George C. Marshall, who later became a full general and served as Chief of Staff organizing the greatest military expansion in U.S. history during WW II. With a relentless push toward the German border during WW I, Tom Sr. and the Allied forces assured victory against Germany on the Western Front.

TW describes his father's position as a machine gunner as *"one of the toughest of all."* Much of his fighting involved fierce trench warfare and frequent shell fire on the front lines. As a result, Tom Sr. lost his hearing during the war. In addition, he survived poison gas attacks and pneumonia (contracted twice) in the mud and trenches of the battlefields of France.

Tom Sr.'s WW I honorable discharge papers and enlistment record, which indicates that he left the United States on June 20, 1918, participated in the battles of Château Thierry (7/25/18), Saint Mihiel (9/12/18), and Meuse-Argonne (9/13/18) and returned home on April 2, 1919. During the period of active combat, the enlistment record notes that Tom Sr. served in the 166th Reg. M.G. (Machine Gun) from 7/22/18 to 1/27/19.

Over sixty-five million soldiers from thirty-six countries fought in WW I, and over nine million of them died as a result. On November 11, 1918, at 11:00 a.m., Germany's defeat was confirmed with an armistice declared between Germany and the United States and its allies. Five months later, Tom Sr. was honorably discharged in April 1919 at twenty-nine years of age.[4]

Reflecting on his father's WW I service, TW adds:

> *Though my father seldom talked about it, I have always taken great pride in his service to his country in WW I.*

President Wilson also took great pride in the service of the American doughboys, exclaiming that they "saved the liberty of the world."

In June 1919, the war was officially ended with the signing of the Versailles peace treaty, which WW I veteran Adolf Hitler later described as "the vilest oppression which peoples and human beings have ever been expected to put up with."[5] Although the world breathed a sigh of relief, some predicted the treaty would not bring lasting peace. One of the French participants in the signing aptly described the treaty as "a twenty-year cease fire." The British Prime Minister similarly bemoaned that "we shall have to do the whole thing again in twenty-five years at three times the cost." Several years later, the war was already being called the "First" World War.

President Wilson declared November 11, 1919, as the first commemoration of "Armistice Day." The following summer, while Republican vice-presidential nominee Calvin Coolidge declared that "the nation which forgets its defenders will itself be forgotten," frustrated artist and WW I veteran Adolf Hitler was busily developing a public brand for his socialist movement using an ancient hooked cross that would later become the feared symbol of the Nazi Party. Although previously used for centuries with positive connotations, the symbol would be forever tainted due to its association with Hitler and his Nazi government, known as the Third Reich. 卐

On November 11, 1921, President Harding officiated at an interment ceremony of an unknown WW I soldier at Arlington Cemetery, the site for which later became known as the Tomb of the Unknown Soldier. The annual commemoration of Armistice Day was changed to "Veterans Day" under President Eisenhower, who in 1958 officiated at the interment of unknown WW II soldiers at Arlington Cemetery. Veterans Day remains a holiday that TW and his family continue to observe faithfully each year in tribute to all American veterans.

---

4   TW also had two uncles who served in WW I, both younger brothers of TW's mother, Allene Thompson Smith. Allene Smith's brother Joseph LeRoy Thompson was wounded in WW I and died from his wounds at Walter Reed Hospital in March 1921 at the age of 28. Another younger brother, Redus Gordon Thompson, was a veteran of both World War I and World War II.

5   Germany made its final reparations payment under the Treaty of Versailles on October 3, 2010.

Tom Sr. was born soon after three other individuals who also fought in France during WW I, each of whom would later have a significant impact on his son's life during WW II.

Harry S. Truman was born on May 8, 1884, in Lamar, Missouri, and was ultimately responsible for making the decision to use the atomic bombs that ended WW II. Truman served as a 34 year old artillery battery commander in the 35th Infantry Division during WW I. Like Tom Sr., Truman fought in Meuse-Argonne and his regiment fired some of the last shots against the Germans during the war. Years later in a 1942 senate speech, Truman referred to WW II as a tragic continuation of "the one we fought in 1917 and 1918."

George Smith Patton, Jr. was born on November 11, 1885, in San Gabriel, California, and was responsible for commanding TW's infantry division in WW II. Patton served as a captain in the U.S. Tank Corps during WW I and, like Tom Sr., fought at Saint Mihiel and Meuse-Argonne. Patton was wounded in 1918 while leading an attack on German machine guns during the first day of the Meuse-Argonne offensive and was given a battlefield promotion to full colonel. Like Tom Sr., many of Patton's relatives fought for the South during the Civil War, and Patton's grandfather, George Smith Patton, Sr., was killed while fighting for the Confederate army in Winchester, Virginia, not far from where Tom Sr.'s grandfather, Albert Henry Smith, was mortally wounded.

Adolf Hitler was born in Austria on April 20, 1889, less than one year before Tom Sr.. The infamous and sadistic Hitler was a root cause of WW II in Europe and countless atrocities. Hitler served in France and Belgium in the 16th Bavarian Reserve Regiment during WW I. Like Tom Sr., Hitler survived poison mustard gas attacks during the war, which he said turned his eyes "into glowing coals" and caused his admission as a "blind cripple" to a field hospital in 1918. Hitler's WW I experiences strongly influenced his Nazi philosophy. In 1922, the year before TW was born, Hitler declared that "It cannot be that 2 million Germans should have fallen in vain. . . . No we do not pardon, we demand vengeance!" Seventeen years later, the former artist had become a captivating orator and would declare in a September 1939 speech, that "[w]hoever fights with poison gas will be fought with poison gas," and that "a November 1918 will never be repeated in German history."

After the war, while receiving medical care at a veterans' hospital for his hearing loss, Tom Sr. received visits from a deaf and blind woman named Helen Keller. Like Tom Sr., Keller's ancestors served in the Confederate army, and the two were surprised to learn of their common upbringing in small towns in northern Alabama. Following a miraculous break-through years earlier with her teacher Annie Sullivan, Keller had become a gifted communicator and dedicated a great deal of time to improving conditions for the deaf and blind. Although outspoken in her opposition to WW I, Helen Keller assisted disabled WW I veterans like Tom Sr. and went on years later to help disabled veterans of WW II.

Despite his hearing loss, Tom Sr. quickly moved on with life. He graduated from the National University Law School, which later merged with the George Washington University Law School. He then went to work for the Department of Justice and later the General Accounting Office, and he was fortunate to have retained steady employment with the government during the great depression of the 1930s. He was even able to afford a $60 Hamilton Elinvar railroad pocket watch, which he bought as a gift for his father, Warner Smith. As one of his last acts from his deathbed, Warner gave the watch back to his son Tom Sr., and Tom Sr. later gave the watch to TW's son, Thomas W. Smith, III.

While attending Alabama Society meetings in Washington, Tom Sr. met Ossie Allene Thompson. Allene, as she was known, was a school teacher from Huntsville, Alabama. She later came to Washington, D.C., to work for the Internal Revenue Service. Tom Sr. and Allene married in the early 1920s, and from that point Allene became known as Allene Thompson Smith.

The name Allene was ironically similar to Tom Sr.'s original middle name of Allen. At birth, Tom Sr.'s parents named him Thomas Allen Smith after a family friend named Allen. Allen went on to become a local drunk and a less than exemplary local citizen. Later in life, Allen put his horses' reins around his neck while drinking and driving his wagon in a standing position. He then fell from the wagon and was dragged to his death. Upon hearing the news of Allen's death, Tom Sr.'s mother crossed out Tom Sr.'s middle name in the family bible, which was the official record at the time, and Tom Sr. never used that middle name again. In fact, Tom Sr. had a tattoo with the initials "TAS" removed from his forearm, although the process was not completely effective, and TW's children recall that you could still see the faint outline of their grandfather's former initials on his forearm.

Perhaps due to the influence of his former namesake, Tom Sr. never drank alcohol but admitted sampling a beer soon after arriving in Washington. TW recalls *my father said he did not like it and didn't understand what all the fuss was about.* As a consequence, the alcohol prohibition era, which lasted from 1920 under President Woodrow Wilson to 1933 under President Franklin Roosevelt, was of little consequence to TW's father.

Tom Sr. and Allene

Tom Sr. and Allene started a family, and Tom Sr. participated in community service events, sang in the choir with other WW I veterans at the Calvary Baptist Church at 8th and H streets, and fulfilled his civic duties as a patriotic American citizen. Consistent with his WW I sacrifices to "make the world safe for democracy," Tom Sr. believed that the privilege of voting in a national election was "something very important," and his sentiments on voting were published in a November 5, 1980 article in the Northern Virginia Sun (facing page). The 90 year old Tom Sr. noted in the article that with the exception of one time when he was overseas during his service in WW I, he had voted in each and every national election since 1911, the first year he was eligible to vote.

Tom Sr. explained in the article that his favorite President was the one he voted for back in 1912 — Woodrow Wilson. Regarding President Wilson, Tom Sr. added that "I liked the way he tried to keep us out of the war, he really made a special effort to keep us out." In the same article, Tom Sr. noted that he personally met President William Howard Taft at the White House in 1922 and that he later met President Calvin Coolidge, who was "tall, skinny and grim," and "looked like he was mad at someone."

FAIRFAX NORTHERN VIRGINIA SUN — Wednesday, November 5, 1980 — Page 2

Tom Smith has been casting his ballot since 1911 and hasn't missed an election. The 1980 sweepstakes were no exception but Smith admits a lot has changed over the past 70 years.
Photo by George Borsley

Things Have Changed For 91-Year-Old Voter

FAIRFAX — Ninety-year-old Thomas Smith has been casting ballots at election time for 69 years and, though he would not reveal his presidential preference this year, he continued that tradition on Tuesday.

The Alabama native first voted on November 2, 1911 in some local contests and moved to the Washington area just 10 days later. After living in the nation's capital for 60 years and working for the federal government, Smith moved to the Falls Church area of the county to live with his son's family.

Smith called the privilege to vote "something very important" in an interview a few hours after he cast his votes Tuesday morning. Since he first registered to vote in 1911 at the age of 21 (which was the minimum age requirement in those days), he said that he has only missed voting day once and that occurred when he was overseas during World War 1.

A lifelong Democrat, he related that his favorite president was the first one he voted for, way back in 1912. Woodrow Wilson was elected that year to the first of two terms as he defeated GOP candidate William Howard Taft and former Republican and Bull Moose Party candidate Teddy Roosevelt.

As for the choice between President-elect Ronald Reagan, President Carter, and independent candidate John Anderson, Smith smiled, "I wouldn't mind going back to Wilson."

"I liked the way he tried to keep us out of war," Smith stated, "he really made a special effort to keep us out."

The U.S. reluctantly entered the first world war toward the end of Wilson's first term after avoiding such participation for over two years.

Roosevelt served as the country's president from 1901 to 1909, and attempted to regain the White House in 1912 as a third party candidate. Historical observers believe that the maverick Republican siphoned off enough votes from Taft to hand the election to Wilson.

When asked how he felt about this chain of events during his first presidential election, he commented, "I thought it was very nice."

Despite voting against President Taft, Smith said that he met the president as he visited the White House in January 1, 1912, and that he has a good lasting impression of the man.

As he and his group were being shown around during the former New Year's tradition, they met Taft and had a brief, "hello, how are you" meeting. "I liked the man," he said.

Smith also related a chance meeting with former President Calvin Coolidge. "I was walking by, looked up and there he was," Smith said. "He looked like he was mad at someone."

Smith, who will soon be 91 in February, described "Silent Cal" as tall, skinny, and grim.

The stately gentleman said that his family had always been Democratic and that was the way many families voted for years. In contrast, his 97-year-old son commented that his family does not adhere to any strict one-party voting, preferring instead to label himself an "independent" thinker.

In addition, Smith pointed also to the fact that when he first voted in 1911, women were not yet allowed to vote. "My mother would not have voted even if she had had the chance," Smith laughed, "since she was too busy already taking care of the children."

The elder Smith's son, Thomas W. Smith, made a final comment: "Sometimes you have to wonder why anybody would want the job," he offered, "since it is so very tough."

The Masonic square and compass insignia on the Washington Masonic National Memorial, 1923.

In 1923, Tom Sr. attended a ceremony during which the cornerstone of the George Washington Masonic National Memorial was laid on Shooter's Hill in Alexandria, Virginia. Among many dignitaries in attendance were President Calvin Coolidge and Freemason and former President Howard Taft, who was at the time Chief Justice of the U.S. Supreme Court. Tom Sr. was a devoted member of the Masonic Fraternity and eventually became a 32nd degree Freemason. He was also an avid supporter of the new memorial to George Washington, who had served as a Charter Master of the Alexandria-Washington lodge and remains a man whom all Freemasons hold with the deepest respect. Unbeknownst to Tom Sr., the peaceful and tolerant Freemason fraternity would be viewed by his former WW I antagonist Adolf Hitler as a threat to his authority, and Freemasons would soon become a target of Hitler's hatred.

Tom Sr. passed away in February 1985 at 95 years of age, and the Freemason square and compass insignia are carved on his tombstone. He lived the last decade of his life with TW, TW's wife Janet, and their five children, Janene, Tommy, Randy, Jennifer and Jefferson, all of whom received direct accounts from Tom Sr. of this history. A rugged Alabama farm native and WW I veteran, Tom Sr. had a gentle, quite demeanor and his grandchildren have many fond memories of him, including his frequent and enthusiastic affirmative response of "Hello Yes."

2. EARLY YEARS

"I survived the depression in time to get in the war."

TW was born at the George Washington University Hospital in Washington, D.C. on July 12, 1923, during the term of U.S. President Calvin Coolidge. During his early years, TW (right) lived with his parents and their dog Puffie ten blocks from the White House in a row house located at 1020 8th Street, N.W., which later became the site of the Washington Convention Center.

From grades K-8, TW attended Sidwell Friends School, where he once danced with a schoolmate named Anne Frances Robbins, later known as First Lady Nancy Reagan. Founded in 1883, the Sidwell Friends School was located at that time in the 1800 block of I Street, just four blocks from the White House and within walking distance of TW's home. Over the years, the school has educated the children of Presidents Theodore Roosevelt, Richard Nixon, William Clinton, and most recently, Barrack Obama. Both Presidents Theodore Roosevelt and William Clinton delivered commencement addresses at the school in 1907 and 1997, respectively.

While attending the Sidwell Friends elementary School, TW walked to school each day, often travelling down Pennsylvania Avenue past the White House. TW vividly recalls seeing First Lady Eleanor Roosevelt at the White House a number of times, including one instance where she said hello.

> *I waved and said hello to Mrs. Roosevelt and she waved and asked how I was doing. She was just returning from a horseback ride, and I was on my way to school.*[6]

6 Eleanor Roosevelt's horse was stabled in Arlington, Virginia, at Fort Meyer, where she also became friends with George Patton's wife, Beatrice.

*TW in front of the family's 1020 8th Street
row house*

TW in a childhood portrait

Tom Sr.'s respect for the U.S. Commander-in-Chief was instilled in his son TW at an early age. To this day, TW can recite every U.S. President in order, remembering the Presidents by single syllables in groups of seven, as learned from his parents and passed on to his own children. Furthermore, TW's grandchildren also remember the Presidents using single syllables as referenced below:

Wash-Ad-Jeff-Mad-Mo-Ad-Jack *Van-Harr-Ty-Po-Tay-Fil-Pierce*

Bu-Linc-John-Grant-Hay-Gar-Art *Cle-Harr-Cle-Mc-Ro-Taft-Wil*

Hard-Cool-Hoo-Ro-Tru-El-Ken *John-Nix-For-Car-Rea-Bush-Clin*

Bush-O-

While growing up in the District of Columbia, TW and his parents attended a number of Presidential Inaugurations, including those of Presidents Herbert Hoover and Franklin Delano Roosevelt. Witnessing such historical events helped TW develop a sense of patriotism and pride in the United States. TW remembers attending one parade in 1929 in honor of President Hoover where the famous John Philip Sousa led a marching band.

TW was born two years after Adolf Hitler became the leader of the Socialist "Nazi" party. Several months after TW's birth, Hitler led a failed attempt in November 1923 to overthrow the German democratic government in an attempted Nazi revolution known as the Beer Hall Putsch. While in prison for treason after his failed revolution, and shortly after TW's second birthday, Hitler published his book called *Mein Kampf* (My Struggle) in July 1925. In *Mein Kampf*, Hitler espoused his views of the Nazi party and his plans for Germany's future and world domination by a superior race. He also warned of the threat of "inferior" races, the perils of freemasonry, a Jewish conspiracy, and the need to avenge Germany's defeat in WW I.

John Philip Sousa was an American composer and conductor who wrote many famous patriotic marching songs, including the U.S. national march song "Stars and Stripes Forever," as well as the Marine Corps' official song "Semper Fidelis," and the Army's "U.S. Field Artillery March." Over forty years earlier, Sousa led the Marine Corps band during the 1881 inauguration of President James Garfield.

TW also recalls that while attending President Hoover's parade, TW's father pointed out an unusual bystander to him:

> *My father pointed to a shabby looking old man who was going through trashcans. The man was picking up trash and searching for tin foil, which I understood he would later try to sell. He was a short elderly white man with a stubby beard, and I remember he was poorly dressed and appeared to be homeless. My father noted that this was the man who as a young boy held the horse for John Wilkes Booth outside Ford's Theater during the assassination of President Lincoln. I understand the man was later scorned by many while others would buy him drinks at local bars.*

The man who held the horse for John Wilkes Booth was named "Peanut" John Burroughs. Following President Lincoln's assassination, Peanut Burroughs testified at the trials of a number of alleged conspirators of John Wilkes Booth. TW understands that the man he saw that day rented a room in a row house near Pennsylvania Avenue, not far from TW's home at the time. Subsequent efforts by TW's children to verify the identity of the man TW saw that day have been unsuccessful because Peanut Burroughs disappeared from the city directory and census reports after 1865.

It is possible that instead of Peanut Burroughs, TW actually saw "Coughdrop Joey" Ratto, who is reported to have lived from 1854 to 1946 and grew up around 10th and E

Streets near Ford's Theater. Coughdrop Joey was a short, colorful figure often seen later in life around the streets and alleys of Ford's Theater where he sold cough drops and pushed around an old wagon cart collecting and selling newspapers. Coughdrop Joey was later incorrectly rumored to have held the horse of John Wilkes Booth. While we may never know for sure who TW saw that day, it is worth noting that TW's father was a well-educated man and had been living in the District for over fifteen years by that point, and only a few blocks away from Ford's Theater. He was convinced, as remains TW, that they saw the man who *"held the horse for John Wilkes Booth."*

In October 1929, during President Hoover's first year in office, the stock market crashed, and the United States, along with many other countries, spiraled into a severe depression. Describing the events leading up to the depression and an underfunded military reduced to 125,000 enlisted men, Harry Truman wrote in his diary that "They began to talk of disarmament. They did disarm themselves, to the point of helplessness. They became fat and rich, special privilege ran the country—ran it to a fall." The great depression left many people homeless and over thirty million Americans without jobs.

TW was attending the Sidwell Friends School during that time and recalls that his parents supplemented their income by renting out the first and third floors of their brownstone row house at 1020 8th Street. TW remembers that many tenants from other row houses in the neighborhood could not make their rent payments and were eventually evicted.

> *You would see all of someone's possessions thrown out on the curb in front of their house. I also recall a great many beggars and homeless people on the streets.*

Perhaps reflecting the hard times of the depression, TW recalls a robbery attempt in which an intruder smashed the bay window of their 8th Street row house and entered the house.

> *My father ran into the room with a pistol and knocked the man unconscious with the butt of his gun. The police arrived and took the man away and we never heard anything more about it.*

During the depression, TW advanced through elementary school and construction progressed on what became known as the George Washington Masonic National Memorial in Alexandria, Virginia. Tom Sr. and his fellow Freemasons raised money for the project, which they paid for entirely with cash. The exterior of the impressive building (opposite page) was completed and an elaborate dedication ceremony and parade were held on May 12, 1932, with thousands of people in attendance. In addition to Army, Navy and Marine Corps bands, Tom Sr. marched in the parade as a flag bearer. TW remembers that his father carried the American flag, noting *"it was a huge flag, but he carried it right along."* President Herbert Hoover attended the dedication ceremony, which included a twenty-one gun salute. TW recalls his parents taking great pride in the new memorial's mission of emulating and promoting "the virtues, character and vision of

The George Washington Masonic National Memorial in Alexandria, Virginia

While the United States struggled through the depression under President Hoover, Germany elected Nazi officials in September of 1930, making the Nazi party the second largest political party in Germany. Like the United States, Germany faced economic troubles and had millions of people out of work, conditions that would provide an opportunity for Hitler and his Nazi leadership to rise to power. Meanwhile, another global threat was developing in the Far East. In 1931, Japan invaded the Chinese province of Manchuria. With a growing population inhabiting an island with limited resources, Japan sought to expand its borders and continued its brutal quest six years later with a full scale attack on the rest of China.

George Washington, the Man, the Mason and Father of our Country." Within two years, the German government began to monitor freemason activities and to compile card catalogs on freemasons and other political and racial enemies, information that would later be used for mass murder.

TW was born at George Washington University Hospital, spent his childhood and career in the first President's namesake city of Washington, D.C., and graduated with undergraduate and law degrees from the George Washington University. George Washington University was started with a bequest from President and Freemason George Washington and the school has strong ties to Freemasonry. In 1821, President and Freemason James Monroe signed the charter for the University, then called Columbian College. In 1904, President and Freemason Theodore Roosevelt restored the school's charter and renamed it George Washington University. Freemasons have donated significant funds and laid many

TW dressed as George Washington for 200th Anniversary of Washington's birthday on February 22, 1932 and for Masonic Memorial Dedication on May 12, 1932.

George Washington statue inside the Masonic Memorial.

of the cornerstones for university buildings, and numerous George Washington University Presidents have been Freemasons. Like his father, TW attended the parade in 1932 honoring George Washington, and the Smith family's pride in President Washington and Tom Sr.'s Masonic Fraternity is apparent in the George Washington costume TW wore.

Fourteen U.S. Presidents were Freemasons, including two Presidents who would have a key impact on WW II—Presidents Franklin Delano Roosevelt and Harry S. Truman. After WW II, Harry Truman dedicated a statue of George Washington at the Masonic Memorial in 1950. TW continues to hold great respect for the Freemasons, and the George Washington Masonic National Memorial remains a source of pride and patriotism to TW.

A few weeks after TW attended the Masonic Memorial dedication, Major George Patton was in Alexandria, Virginia, delivering a speech to the American Legion on Memorial Day, 1932. With an army that was ranked a dismal seventeenth in the world, Patton passionately denounced pacifists who were "constantly working to change Armistice

Day into disarmament day," and whose belief in "perpetual peace" was "a futile dream." Patton exclaimed that if America did not remain prepared for war, the many lives sacrificed during WW I would have been in vain.

The depression was difficult for TW's family and friends, and TW also remembers the impacts of the hard times on many WW I veterans. Shortly after TW's ninth birthday and about two months after the preceding photo of TW was taken, TW's father took him down to the Capitol during the summer of 1932 to see a gathering of a group of WW I veterans who called themselves the Bonus Expeditionary Force. The Bonus Expeditionary Force was comprised of approximately 15,000 largely unemployed and disgruntled WW I veterans seeking immediate payment of a promised WW I bonus of $1.25 per day served overseas and $1.00 per day served in the United States. Congress approved the bonus in 1924, well before the Depression, however the payment was not due until 1945.

Most of the Bonus Expeditionary Force stayed in a makeshift camp at Anacostia Flats, which some called "Hooverville," from which they led marches on the Capitol for over a month, at times including up to 40,000 people. Following the Senate's rejection of their demands, many veterans, with nowhere else to go, stayed in their camps and continued their marches, resulting in a tense environment on Capitol Hill.

On July 28, 1932, the Attorney General ordered the evacuation of the Bonus Expeditionary Force from all government property. After a confrontation with D.C. police resulted in two shooting deaths, President Hoover dispatched U.S. Army tanks, infantry and cavalry in what would be the military's only action during the period leading up to WW II. Under the leadership of General Douglas MacArthur, Major Dwight Eisenhower served as police liaison and Major George Patton led the cavalry. Among the veterans confronted by Major Patton during the evacuation was Joe Angelo, who had received a Distinguished Service Cross for saving Patton's life during WW I. Although disapproving of the bonus marchers, Patton later described the Bonus March evacuation as "a most distasteful form of service." With troops brandishing bayonets and tear gas, and a stunned group of WW I veterans thinking initially that the military was dispatched to help them, the veteran protesters were dispersed by nightfall and their camps were burned.

TW still remembers the event, often referred to as the "Bonus March":

> It was an unbelievable scene. A lot of people were bitter about the bonus. My father was sympathetic with the marchers, and we went downtown to watch them. They were everywhere and jammed up everything. During one march, trucks arrived with GIs and police from Fort Myer to chase them away. Soldiers jumped out with rifles and bayonets. I understand a couple people were killed.

TW's childhood friend Dave Bell, who would later depart with TW for WW II, lived in Cleveland Park and watched the fleeing marchers on Wisconsin Avenue. Bell also remembers the event:

I'd never seen such a sorry looking crowd in my life. My Dad told me they had given a lot for our country and were treated poorly. He said I should clap for them as they go by, and that is what I did.

The Bonus Expeditionary Force left Washington without their WW I bonuses, but their efforts were not in vain. They had successfully raised awareness in the public and political eye, and Congress would consider the bonus again a few years later. Fortunately for TW, the Bonus March would later prove to be a contributing factor in the adoption of the 1944 GI Bill of Rights, which paid for TW to receive undergraduate and law degrees after WW II.

The Bonus March also proved to be a factor in President Hoover's election defeat, and in 1932, Franklin Delano Roosevelt was elected to the first of four terms as President of the United States. Still nine years of age, TW and his parents went back to the Capitol to see Franklin Roosevelt's inauguration ceremony in March of 1933. In his inaugural address, the newly elected President acknowledged that "only a foolish optimist can deny the dark realities of the moment," but also exclaimed that "the only thing we have to fear is fear itself."

As President Roosevelt prepared for the Presidency, Adolf Hitler became Chancellor of Germany in January 1933 and later assumed dictatorial power under the Enabling Act in March 1933. Also in March, the Nazis opened the Dachau concentration camp near Munich, Germany, where they imprisoned and tortured political opponents and Jews, as well as Freemasons, who were forced to wear inverted red triangle patches. In April, the Nazis began a boycott of Jewish merchants. In May 1933, while TW learned about American history and recited the pledge of allegiance each day at the Sidwell Friends School, German citizens sang Nazi anthems, placed copies of *Mein Kampf* on church altars, required children to swear allegiance to Hitler Youth organizations, and burned books with "un-German" ideas. On May 17, 1933, Hitler delivered his "Peace Speech," exclaiming that "Germany would also be perfectly ready to disband her entire military establishment and destroy the small amount of arms remaining to her, if the neighboring countries would do the same." Two months later, the Nazi party was declared the sole political party in Germany. During the same year, Hitler established the German secret police known as the Gestapo. The Nazis continued to terrorize Jews by enacting race laws that stripped the Jews of their rights. By the end of 1933, more than fifty concentration camps were built as Hitler moved toward his quest for "the annihilation of the Jewish race in Europe." A year later, the Nazis murdered Austria's Chancellor and continued covert war preparation while publicly talking about peace.

In May 1933, the Bonus Expeditionary Force marched on Washington again. President Roosevelt sent First Lady Eleanor Roosevelt to meet with the veterans for coffee, and she was successful in persuading many of them to sign up for work with one of President Roosevelt's New Deal projects called the Civilian Conservation Corps ("CCC"). The CCC was created to put young men to work while at the same time conserving the nation's natural resources. Operated by General Douglas MacArthur, the program left a long legacy of park and conservation projects in every state in the country.

TW's uncle Redus Thompson, a veteran of WW I and later WW II, worked for the CCC building roads and culverts and cleaning up Civil War battlefields in Fredericksburg, Virginia. While working on the battlefields with the boys of the CCC, Redus found Civil War relics, including a bayonet, a Union Army belt buckle, and dozens of Confederate and Union army bullets, which he gave to TW and which TW possesses to this day.

In addition to his Civil War relics, TW's interest in history at a young age is also apparent from the newspaper clipping from the November 1934 *Washington Daily News*. The newspaper clipping contains a picture of TW at eleven years of age holding a newspaper dated 1838, along with a caption that read:

"Tom Smith, 11, found a bound volume of the Portsmouth, Va., Old Dominion published nearly 100 years ago, while he was rummaging thru some trash near his home at 1020 Eighth St., NW. Copies of the old paper, printed in 1838, include advertisements for runaway slaves, and a series of vigorous editorials against the Whig Party. *Washington Daily News*, November 1934"

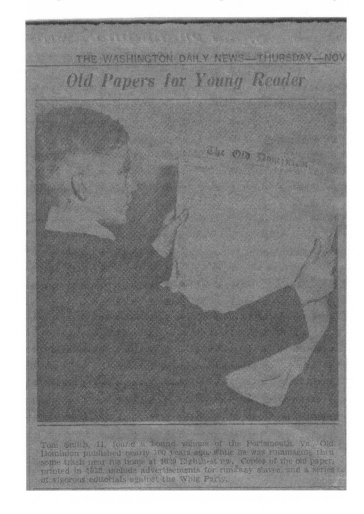

THE WASHINGTON DAILY NEWS—THURSDAY—NOV

Old Papers for Young Reader

Tom Smith, 11, found a bound volume of the Portsmouth, Va., Old Dominion published nearly 100 years ago, while he was rummaging thru some trash near his home at 1020 Eighth-st nw. Copies of the old paper, printed in 1838, include advertisements for runaway slaves, and a series of vigorous editorials against the Whig Party.

In 1838, when TW's edition of *The Old Dominion* newspaper was printed, the country was similarly in the midst of a depression that included bank failures and record unemployment levels. The Whig political party referenced in the article had recently been formed, largely in opposition to President Andrew Jackson's policies. Whig party candidate William Henry Harrison was elected President two years later in 1840, serving for only thirty-one days before becoming the first President to die in office. The abhorrent practice of slavery, also referenced in TW's 1838 Old Dominion Newspaper article, was one of the contributing causes of a Civil War that would absorb the country twenty years later. Although TW's ancestors joined the fight on behalf of their Southern homeland, TW believes his ancestors to have been of modest means and he is aware of no evidence that they were among the estimated seventeen percent of Southern white inhabitants who owned slaves.

In 1935, a year after the *Washington Daily News* photograph of TW was published, President Roosevelt visited The Citadel in South Carolina. After praising the "great historic tradition of that school—an historical record, a war record, if you please, of the Citadel boys that ought to be known to every boy in the United States," Roosevelt explained that:

> Yes, we are on our way back—not just by pure chance, my friends, not just by a turn of the wheel, of the cycle. We are coming back more soundly than ever before because we are planning it that way. Don't let anybody tell you differently. . . . There are many grave problems ahead. As you know, I spoke in San Diego, in California, three weeks ago today. I spoke in regard to the affairs of the world and I tried to make it clear then, as I continue to make it clear today, that it shall be my earnest effort to keep this country free and unentangled from any possible war that may occur across the seas.

On Labor Day in 1935, over 250 WW I veterans working with the CCC on the construction of a highway to the Florida Keys were killed in a horrific hurricane, and public sentiment continued to grow in support of the WW I veterans who had sacrificed for their country. By 1936, with many members of Congress facing re-election, Congress approved an early award of the nearly $2 billion in WW I bonuses that the Bonus Expeditionary Force had sought four years earlier. President Roosevelt vetoed the legislation, but Congress mustered enough votes to over-ride the veto. TW's father and the rest of the WW I veterans received their bonus money the same year, and TW still remembers how the family used the money.

> *After my dad received the WW I bonus money, my parents used some of it for a car trip out West. We visited many sites, including Yellowstone Park, Pikes Peak, and the Alamo. We also stopped to see relatives in Alabama.*

TW (third from right) and his parents (right) at Pikes Peak, Colorado

Two days before his 13th birthday, and less than a month before an African-American track star named Jesse Owens won four gold medals before a shocked and disappointed Adolf Hitler at the summer Olympic games in Berlin, TW posed for a picture with his parents on the family trip out West, funded by the WW I bonus that Tom Sr. received early, compliments of the Bonus Expeditionary Force.

TW graduated from Sidwell Friends Elementary School in 1937. During the same year, President Roosevelt began his second term of office and U.S. soldiers began a 24/7 guard of the Tomb of the Unknown Soldier at Arlington Cemetery. Following graduation from elementary school, TW attended a small high school in the District of Columbia called the Woodward School for Boys. Located in the YMCA building at 1736 G Street, the Woodward school had less than 150 students, and TW knew most of them, including Dave Bell, who was one year behind TW. TW and Dave Bell would later join the Army together and the two boys would become lifelong friends. During this period, Dave Bell remembers his father returning from a trip to Germany in 1937:

> He told me that he could feel that war was coming. He said the Germans were very militaristic and were arming themselves to the teeth.

TW and his parents moved to a house at 5436 32nd Street, N.W., Washington, D.C. where TW also became good friends with three neighborhood boys who lived several houses away. Like TW, John Beall, Paul Dietrick and Harold Moynelo would each later go off to fight in WW II, and TW recalls with anguish that *"they never came home."*

For his own income during this period of the depression, TW remembers working one summer for the Department of Agriculture.

I earned 27 cents an hour and paid 3 cents to ride the streetcar. I was later delighted to be promoted and earn $3 per diem, WAE. WAE meant "when actually employed," meaning I was not paid for holidays or time off.

Reflecting years later on these times, TW explains:

I survived the Depression in time to get in the war.

As the United States began to emerge from the Depression, Hitler's Nazi Germany relentlessly continued its reign of oppression as it sought to advance a supreme German race and to expand the Nazi empire following its losses in 1918. After annexing Austria under the guise of a "liberator," Hitler declared in 1938 that "my patience is now at an end." He successfully negotiated with France and England for Germany's annexation of Sudetenland, an action that Winston Churchill described as "a total and unmitigated defeat" and "a disaster of the first magnitude." This success caused a jubilant Hitler to exclaim that "I will go down as the greatest German in history." In 1939, Germany signed a "Pact of Steel" with Italy, forming an alliance that Italian Dictator Benito Mussolini described as an "axis" around which other countries would work. Germany also continued to oppress and imprison political opponents and races deemed inferior, began to euthanize the sick and disabled, and invaded Poland. In 1940, when TW entered his final year at the Woodward School for Boys, Germany was invading and attacking countries throughout Europe. Germany attacked England, which Hitler predicted would "force England to her knees." Germany invaded Denmark, Luxembourg, Romania and the Netherlands, and forced the surrender of Holland, Belgium and Norway. Germany invaded France, causing it to surrender and General Charles de Gaulle to flee to London, later declaring "[t]oday we are crushed by the sheer weight of mechanized force hurled against us." Italy, as well, invaded Greece, Egypt and other areas of North Africa in 1940. The Axis Powers of Germany, Italy and Japan, each seeking to expand their empires, solidified their unity in September of 1940 by signing the Tripartite Pact. They were soon joined by Hungary and Romania, and later Bulgaria. By April 1941, as TW prepared for his high school graduation and President Roosevelt was beginning his third term in office, Yugoslavia and Greece surrendered to the Nazis. Several months later, Germany invaded Russia.

At the Woodward School for Boys, TW participated in soccer and swimming, and was also an active member of the debate team. Dave Bell recalled that TW was "argumentative and loved to debate, which later made him a good lawyer." During his final semester at the Woodward School in 1941, TW won a key debate, earning him the title "Woodward's Outstanding Debater." The topic of the debate was foreign threats to the United States. With perhaps a surprising premonition of things to come, TW argued less than a year before Pearl Harbor that Japan posed the greatest global threat.

In recognition of TW's victory, the school principal, James J. King, gave TW a book in June 1941 entitled *Blood Sweat, and Tears*. The book is a collection of speeches made by British Prime Minister Winston S. Churchill during the period from May 1938 to February 1941. Compiled by Winston Churchill's son, Randolph S. Churchill, the speeches provide what Randolph Churchill described as "a running commentary upon the remorseless deterioration of the foreign situation" and a "last word upon the war." On the book's inside cover, Principal King wrote a note to TW:

> The Special Award to Thomas Warner Smith, Woodward's Outstanding Debater for 1941! My hearty congratulations to you. It is my hope that this stirring book will be an added inspiration to you in your continued growth and development. You are on the way. Keep up the good work. Cordially your friend, James J. King, June 16, 1941

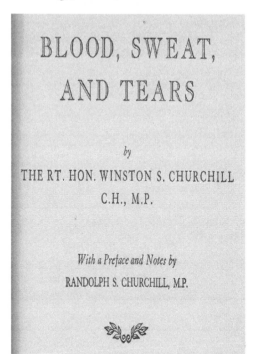

The "stirring book" of WW II speeches was indeed an inspiration to TW, including Prime Minister Churchill's January 9, 1941, observation that:

> It is no exaggeration to say that the future of the whole world and the hopes of a broadening civilization founded upon Christian ethics depend upon the relations between the British Empire or Commonwealth of Nations and the USA.

and the Prime Minister's February 9, 1941, declaration that:

> We shall not fail or falter; we shall not weaken or tire. Neither the sudden shock of battle, nor the long-drawn trials of vigilance and exertion will wear us down.

In a college history paper that TW wrote the following year, TW described the book as a must read. Although noting in the paper that *"I had to spend half my time looking up words in the dictionary,"* TW predicted that *"many histories of this time will be written but none will be better than Blood, Sweat & Tears."* Ultimately TW drew a paramount conclusion from the book:

> *The one thing that shines clear through all of these speeches is the conviction that a truce with Nazism means the ultimate death of freedom for the world.*

3. THE CITADEL, PEARL HARBOR AND
OFF TO THE RECRUITING STATION

"The Marine Corps recruiting station was jammed with people—
we couldn't even get in the door."

TW (center) carrying flag   TW at the Citadel

After graduation from high school at the Woodward School for Boys in 1941, TW elected to enroll at the Citadel, the military college of South Carolina in Charleston. Following its founding in 1842 with a goal of preparing men for "any station or condition of life," Citadel graduates had served their country in all of the nation's conflicts, and the Citadel cadet corps had the distinction of firing the first shots of the Civil War. Indeed, the historic "War Between the States" began nearly twenty years after the Citadel's founding, when Citadel Cadet G. E. Haynsworth fired on the Union ship "Star of the West" on January 9, 1861. With a great grandfather who served in the Civil War under a Citadel graduate, TW's decision to attend a military college during what later would become known as the "War Years" is consistent with and perhaps influenced by his family history of military service.

While attending the Citadel, TW was active in a number of clubs including (1) the International Relations club, in which students of politics discussed topics of national and international significance, (2) the Calliopean Literary Society, which included public speaking and debate and the opportunity to discuss current topics of interest, and (3) the Sons of the American Legion, the Citadel chapter of which was founded only a few years earlier. With pride in his father's WW I service, TW was pleased to join the Citadel Chapter of the Sons of the American Legion, the membership of which included sons of WW I veterans who wished to foster a true spirit of Americanism, as further explained in the yearbook page (opposite page).

In the Fall of 1941, while TW endured his humbling first year as a Citadel "knob," the Nazis ordered all Jews to wear yellow stars and began to experiment with gas chambers at Auschwitz. On September 29, 1941, the Nazis murdered over 33,000 Jews at Kiev. Germany made significant advances into almost all of Europe, but Britain's Royal Air Force continued valiantly to defend against intense German bombing. Just three years earlier, former British Prime Minister Chamberlain had negotiated a 1938 pact with Hitler and predicted "peace in our time." However, by October 1941 it was anything but, and British Prime Minister Winston Churchill exclaimed that England must "Never give in. Never give in. Never, never, never, never—in nothing, great or small, large or petty—never give in, except to convictions of honor and good sense. Never yield to force. Never yield to the apparently overwhelming might of the enemy." During this period, Germany also was advancing into Russia and North Africa. While President Roosevelt and General George Marshall's foremost concern was the pressing threat of Nazi Germany, another Axis Power and German ally, Japan, posed an increasing threat to the United States. Despite General Marshall's belief that the Japanese "wouldn't dare attack Hawaii," and Navy Secretary Frank Knox's December 4, 1941, affirmation that "no matter what happens the U.S. Navy is not going to be caught napping," Japan was aggressively planning an attack on the United States at Pearl Harbor in order to prevent any interference with Japanese empire expansion. During the same period, the United States was contemplating whether to initiate an atomic weapon project that would later be instrumental in the United States' relations with Japan. Consideration of the project began years earlier while TW was still in high school, following President Roosevelt's receipt of a letter dated August 2, 1939 from a prominent Jewish scientist named Albert Einstein. Having fled Nazi Germany and emigrated to the United States six years earlier, Einstein urged the Administration to support the development of an atomic bomb before Germany does so first.

TW in second row, fifth from right.

"To foster and perpetuate a true spirit of American-ism . . ." is the purpose for which the Citadel Chapter of the Sons of the American Legion was established. The Citadel Squadron was founded in 1938 under the direction of Charleston Post No. 10 of the American Legion, with the distinction of being the original chapter of the national organization founded in a college or university.

Any cadets who are sons of veterans of the first World War are eligible for membership. The squadron was founded to provide an organization in order that cadets whose fathers fought in any branch of the American armed forces during the last war might meet and have informal discussions. Programs each year consist of interesting talks by veterans of the war, or by cadets who are associated with the organization.

THE SONS OF THE AMERICAN LEGION

Also during his first year, TW became best of friends with his first year roommate, Charlie Forrest, who was from Anderson, South Carolina. Charlie Forrest would also join the army and fight in WW II, landing in Normandy on D-Day. Like TW, Charlie fought in Germany in the Battle of the Bulge, and the two boys became lifelong friends.

TW (left) and Forrest

On Sunday morning, December 7, 1941, at 7:55 am, Japan launched a devastating attack on Pearl Harbor, during which 353 Japanese aircraft sank or damaged eight U.S. battleships, three cruisers, three destroyers, one minelayer and 188 aircraft. As a result of the attack, 2,390 people were killed and hundreds more wounded. Many of the fatalities occurred on the USS Arizona, which was hit at 8:06 am by a nearly two ton bomb that hit the ship's ammunition magazine, causing it to sink in less than nine minutes along with 1,177 crew members.

TW was an 18 year-old freshman at the Citadel when Japan attacked Pearl Harbor and was walking home from church that Sunday afternoon when he heard cadets yelling about the attack. TW heard further details on the radio. TW's 1942-1943 centennial edition of the Citadel yearbook, *The Sphinx*, recorded the sentiments of the day:

> It was a Sunday afternoon. Most of the cadets were sleeping, or listening to the music on the radio when the reports started coming in. "Pearl Harbor bombed." "Japanese attack the Philippines." The news was received with surprising calmness, as if it had been expected. That night we marched to supper chanting "Beat Japan" to the rhythm of the old Bulldog cadence. The Citadel was once again to have its full share in the fight for human liberties. We were ready. We wanted to go out at once, but we were finally convinced that we should stay and finish our training.

TW's friend Dave Bell was in his final year of high school and was attending a Redskins football game at Griffith Stadium in Washington, D.C., that day. Despite frequent announcements asking military personnel to report to their offices, the Redskins team president did not want Redskins fans to be distracted and would not allow an announcement about the attack, which had started an hour before the 2:00 pm kickoff [2:00 pm

Eastern time was 9:00 am in Hawaii]. With Sammy Baugh at quarterback, the Redskins beat the Eagles 20-14, but the jubilation was short-lived. Bell learned of the attack on his way down the stadium's exit ramps, and remembers that "it sobered everyone up in a hurry."

Although TW recalls reading of President Roosevelt's reference to "a date which will live in infamy," he and Dave Bell may not have fully appreciated the profound impact of that day on the rest of their lives.

The United States declared war on Japan on December 8, 1941. British Prime Minister Churchill heard the welcome news from President Roosevelt that "we're all in the same boat now," after which Churchill "slept the sleep of the saved and thankful." During the week following the attack on Pearl Harbor and President Roosevelt's declaration that "the American people in their righteous might will win through to absolute victory," TW went down with a few cadets to a Marine Corps recruiting station and sought to enlist in the Marine Corps. TW recalls that *"The Marine Corps station was jammed with people—we couldn't even get in the door."* The Marine Corps told TW and his friends the corps was at capacity and they should come back another time.

TW remembers a patriotic fervor that overcame the nation, consistent with President Roosevelt's earlier fireside chats exclaiming that "we are all in it together—all the way," that "every single man, woman, and child is a partner in the most tremendous undertaking in our American history," and that "we must be the great arsenal of democracy." TW still sings songs from the time, and having just visited the Alamo five years earlier, specifically recalls and still enjoys singing the words to "Remember Pearl Harbor:"

Let's REMEMBER PEARL HARBOR,
As we go to meet the foe,
Let's REMEMBER PEARL HARBOR,
As we did the Alamo.

We will always remember,
how they died for liberty,
Let's REMEMBER PEARL HARBOR,
and go on to victory.

On the same day as the bombing of Pearl Harbor, Japan invaded Siam and Malaya. Following the United States' declaration of war, the United States joined Great Britain and Soviet Russia in an alliance called the Allied Powers. A few days later, Germany and Italy joined Japan in declaring war on the United States. Later that month, Japan invaded Hong Kong, soon followed by invasions of the Philippines, Burma and Java.

TW at the Citadel

TW also has fond memories of a song entitled "Praise the Lord and Pass the Ammunition." TW continued his training and studies at the Citadel that first year while also reading about WW II battles such as Wake Island and Corregidor.

In his second year at the Citadel, TW was joined by Dave Bell. Bell was a year behind TW and upon arriving as a freshman knob was relieved that "at least I had one friend at that damned school."

Dave Bell

On December 1, 1942, while a sophomore at the Citadel, the 19-year old TW went to the military recruiting station along with his buddy Dave Bell and a number of other cadet friends. TW and Bell decided to join the Army, which had the longest line of the military branches. The Army accepted TW and Bell and swore them in.

TW was not alone in his desire to join the fight in WW II. The Citadel's website notes that:

> During World War II, among the nations, colleges, and universities, The Citadel had the distinction of having the highest percentage of its students enter military service with the single exception of the national service academies. Of 2,976 living graduates in 1946, 1,927 had served their country (66%), with the same estimated percentage of alumni (non-graduates) having served as well. Indeed, only two members from the famous class of 1944 actually graduated as the entire class was called to arms, or enlisted in military service.

On Christmas day, December 25, 1942, TW's parents gave him a new Movado watch. The watch is engraved:

Thomas W. Smith, From Mother and Dad, 12-25-42

TW wore this watch every day during WW II and still wears the watch to this day.

During the months leading up to TW's enlistment, German atrocities continued, including mass murders at Auschwitz, deportations from the Warsaw Ghetto and the opening of the Treblinka extermination camp in 1942. In April 1942, tens of thousands of U.S. and Filipino troops on Bataan surrendered to the Japanese in the Philippines, only to suffer physical torture, scorching heat, and starvation. Thousands of troops died on the sixty mile "Bataan Death March" through Philippine jungles. During the same month, Lieutenant Colonel James Doolittle led an air raid on Japanese home cities, causing modest damage but significant embarrassment to the Japanese government, which promptly executed three captured American airmen. In May, U.S. troops on Corregidor in the Philippines surrendered to the Japanese. In June, the U.S. defeated the Japanese in the battle of Midway. In August, the U.S. Army Corps of Engineers commenced the top secret Manhattan Project to develop the atomic bomb. Several months later the U.S. and other Allied Forces invaded North Africa.

After Christmas, TW began what, unbeknownst to him, would be his last semester at the Citadel.   In March 1943, TW attended the Citadel's Centennial Celebration, which although substantially curtailed due to the war efforts, still included parades and cadet paratroopers. Two months later, TW finished his second year at the Citadel. Along with other underclassmen from the "War Years," TW and Dave Bell purchased Citadel class rings. The rings did not include the year of graduation, and the school's unprecedented action of providing the rings before the year of graduation was based on the recognition that many of the cadets would never return. TW also received his personal edition of the centennial edition Citadel yearbook, *The Sphinx*, which noted:

> The year 1942 has been recorded in the annals of time as a year in which the world was witness to some of the most tragic events that have marred our modern civilized efforts. The highlight of this particular year was the war, and all our efforts were directed toward the successful conclusion of that war. Events which had seemed to be of major importance were forced into the background: so "all out" was our effort. We were fighting for the survival of our democracy, our democratic institutions, and the belief that God had created man to be free in body and spirit rather than a slave to a demagogue. . . .

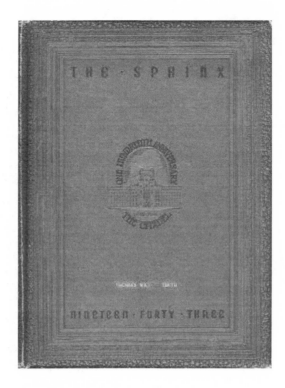

The stirring part that The Citadel is playing in the war is the climax to a century of progress. "Down Through The Years" from 1842 to 1942, one can see a tiny spark that has grown into a tremendous flame whose light is ever shedding its brilliance throughout the world. . . A living, growing symbol of America's true spirit, The Citadel stands in name and edifice as an institution dedicated to freedom and democracy.

TW said what would be his final good byes to many of his classmates. Among those signing his yearbook was his good friend and roommate Charlie Forrest. Other entries in TW's yearbook include:

Best of luck to a swell guy with the best sense of humor I've seen. Bill Barnes

Lots of luck to a damn good fellow. W.R. Affleck

From one Alabama boy to another. It's been nice knowing you "T". Best of luck. Runk James

Charlie Forrest

I shall always cherish the memories I have of my most dearest friend, Tom Smith. Write me, Tom and I shall do the same. Your <u>very</u> best Pal, Charlie.

Best wishes to one of the swellest fellows I know. See you in the army. Holman W. Jenkins.

Good luck to you boy. I've enjoyed knowing you this year even if you're an infantryman. Best wishes, Ed Manion

It's been a pleasure being your old lad for a year. I'll always remember you as a true blooded southerner. Ernest Prevost

Here's hoping the best of luck to a damn good looking boy. W.C. Watson

In my estimation you are a swell fellow and a damn good cadet. D.B. Crosby.

Best of luck always to a really swell A company fellow. Your pal, Harry Ellinor

Best of luck to a damn swell fellow. You certainly would have been successful if the Axis hadn't come around. Otis Baughman.

While at the Citadel, TW was assigned to A Company, which included two of TW's good friends, a senior named Jack Schnibben and a freshman named Harry Launius. Both boys signed TW's yearbook and were later killed in 1945 fighting in Germany where TW would also fight. TW's yearbook contains many dozens of names that he later marked with a red X, denoting that they were killed during the war, including the pictures of his friends Jack Schnibben and Harry Launius on the following page.

Martin Frederick ("Jack") Schnibben, Jr.   *Harry Bell Launius, Jr.*

In July of 1943, TW packed his bag and prepared to leave for the war with Dave Bell. The two young men posed for a picture on the porch of TW's house at 5436 32nd Street. While TW's parents' nerves are perhaps apparent from the less than perfect centering of the picture, Dave Bell recalls that "we weren't afraid or apprehensive at all; we thought it was an adventure and didn't have the vaguest idea of what we were in for." TW, wearing his new Movado watch, also posed for a picture while getting into the car for the drive to the train station.

TW's mother and father dropped TW and David Bell off at D.C.'s Union Station, not far from where the two boys attended high school together. As in WW I, Union Station was a busy place during WW II, and in 1942 *Parade* magazine observed that "under its vaulted roof is staged the whole drama of a nation at war." At Union Station, the boys posed for one more set of pictures before boarding a train for Camp Lee, Virginia.

As noted by TW's friend, the Reverend Charles Manning, 94th Infantry Division, 301st Regiment, Company H, speaking at a 94th Division Association reunion in 1995:

> On December 7, 1941, America found herself involved in World War II, and she was instantly inundated with horrendous problems, one of which was how to transform a happy-go-lucky, twenty-year old, mommy's boy into a Man O'War in thirteen weeks.

TW (left) and Dave Bell　　　　*TW*

TW with his parents at Union Station　　　*TW (left) and Dave Bell at Union Station*

4. ARMY TRAINING AND THE 94TH INFANTRY DIVISION

"At the time I held the most important position in the Army – Pfc. Infantry Rifleman (Patton's Third Army)"

War training was an intensive process designed to include proficiency tests, thirteen weeks of individual training, five weeks of unit training, four weeks of combined training, seven weeks of maneuvers, and six weeks of post-maneuver training. War training would prove critical against formidable Axis opponents, of whom Hitler demanded:

> Close your hearts to pity! Act brutally!. . . Be harsh and remorseless! Be steeled against all signs of compassion!. . . Whoever has pondered over this world order knows that its meaning lies in the success of the best by means of force.

TW reported first to Camp Lee, Virginia, on July 15, 1943. After arriving, TW and Dave Bell recall an onslaught of yelling and orders, and TW still remembers his first communication with the reception center:

> *I told them I wanted to be in the Rainbow Division like my father, and they told me to Shut Up!*

Soon after arriving, TW sent his parents the postcard below:

Rc. C. 1   RECRUITS ARRIVING AT RECEPTION CENTER—CAMP LEE, VA.

On the back of the postcard, TW wrote a short note to his parents addressed from Pvt. Thomas W. Smith:

> *Dear Mother and Dad,*
>
> *Am here and alright. Get my uniform, exams and shots tomorrow. The food is fine and I am having a good time.*
> > *your son,*
> > *Tom*

Upon arriving at Camp Lee, TW remembers his first assignment:

> *After being given a uniform and vaccinations I was assigned to K.P. at 4:45 pm. I soon learned that K.P (Kitchen Police) was not law enforcement. My assignment involved slicing bacon and bread and scrubbing tables and floors until about 5:00 A.M.*

A few days later, TW sent his parents the postcard below with a postmark of July 21, 1943.

FITTING SHOES—RECEPTION CENTER—CAMP LEE, VA.

On the back of the postcard, TW wrote:

> *Dear Mother & Dad,*
>
> *I am still down here but will probably leave any day now. Got Pros & Weekley's letters. Lived through K.P. with no ill effects. Everything is all right and I am fine.*
> > *your son,*
> > *Tom*

By July of 1943, the U.S. had captured Guadalcanal from the Japanese, the Axis Forces had surrendered in North Africa, Nazi troops had crushed Jewish resistance in the Warsaw Ghetto uprising killing thousands of Jews, the Allies had landed in Sicily, and President Roosevelt had announced that the war could only end with Germany's unconditional surrender.

A short time later, TW sent his parents a third postcard (below) with a July 24, 1943 postmark.

TYPICAL CHAPEL SURROUNDED BY BARRACKS—CAMP LEE, VA.

On the back of the postcard, TW wrote:

Dear Mother & Dad,

A man promised me a ride and I have applied for a week-end pass. It is not at all certain that I will make it though. Don't rely on this but I might get home Saturday evening. Am feeling fine. Maybe I will see you soon.

> *your son,*
> *Tom*

TW was fortunate in finding a ride home that weekend, where he posed with his parents in Washington, D.C., for a last picture before leaving for more training and eventually off to war.

TW with his Mother and Father

Soon thereafter, the Army sent TW and Dave Bell by train to Camp Hood, Texas, for basic training. Unfortunately, TW's first brush with a GI casualty occurred at Camp Hood, many months before he would see combat action.

> *After a long ride we got off at North Camp Hood, Texas. There I was assigned to a bunk in a tar paper shack called a barracks. Briefly met the boy in the bunk next to mine. He said his name was Higgins and that before being called to active duty he had been a student at Notre Dame University. Before we could get unpacked a sergeant came in and selected ten men for work detail. The last one selected was Higgins. I would have been next. The work detail left but Higgins never came back. Nearby they were building new barracks and dynamite had been placed in the ground to break it up. The men on the work detail were to shovel up the broken ground. Apparently one of the dynamite charges failed to explode when ignited. Higgins shovel must have hit the dynamite and it exploded killing him.*

One of the boys selected for the work detail assignment was TW's friend Gus Stavros. Stavros was from New Jersey and had been a student at Columbia University. Like TW, he was later assigned to the 94th Infantry Division. In a 2009 oral history, Stavros recalled that after being assigned to the work detail team, he was one of two people on the team who fortunately volunteered for a separate mess hall assignment. Although his recollection of the location and other details differed somewhat from TW's some sixty-four years later, Stavros recounted his understanding of what happened:

TW (center, front row) and friends at Camp Hood. TW's friend Graham Northrup is kneeling in the first row on the left. TW's friend Chuck Meyers is kneeling in the first row on the right. T. Hopper is standing on the right.

We had quite an entry into the infantry. . . . We were to dig a latrine at the officers' mess. [The Sergeant said] two of you can volunteer to be in the mess hall for the officers. Well you know they say you're not to volunteer, but my gosh, I grew up in my father's diner and I said I'll volunteer. … A Sergeant would go in and put two charges in, set them off, and then one of the trainees would go with a pick and another with a shovel, pick and shovel, and they'd work for ten minutes and then the next two would go and do the same thing. And then he'd put in two more charges. What happened was that one time there was only one explosion. So the sergeant went and checked, looked around and couldn't find it. He said they must have gone off together. So the first fellas went in, pick and shovel for ten minutes. And then the next group went and picked, he hit the charge, killed him immediately and his partner was blinded for life.

Reflecting on the incident Stavros added "So, you know, life is full of experiences like this. I could have been there, but I wasn't." Dave Bell, who was in a nearby barracks and also still recalls the incident, adds:

Camp Hood was a dreadful place. We were in Texas in the middle of the summer. It was 110 degrees and boys were dropping like flies. In addition to the dynamite incident, I remember that seven or eight people died from heat exhaustion.

TW recalls rigorous training at Camp Hood, which included a rifle range *"with the old [WW I] Lee Enfield rifle"*, and an infiltration course, and TW has *"particularly fond memories of 25-mile hikes with full field equipment."* TW further remembers that it was at Camp Hood that he had his first exposure to his German opponents.

TW at Camp Hood

> *All of my time at Camp Hood was spent in drill, rifle, bayonet and combat training. Nearby was a German Prisoner of War camp. Most of them were from Rommel's Africa Corps. They were very impressive. The smallest one was about six foot two and must have weighed over two hundred pounds. They were all neat and trim. A friend of mine said that "If these surrendered, what must the ones be like that are still mad?" I didn't need to hear that.*

TW also recalls that while he and other GIs trained each day near the German prison camp, one of the prisoners jeered at the GIs, saying "what is this some kind of circus."

Meanwhile, General George Patton, who fought with Tom Sr. in WW I, was in Sicily, where he openly discouraged his men from taking prisoners, demanding instead that they "build up that name as killers." In August 1943, Patton was involved in two incidents in Sicily that would later have an impact on TW. Having advanced to the rank of General since breaking up the Bonus March that TW watched ten years earlier, Patton was obsessed about his combat destiny and heritage, leading aggressive battles in North Africa and Sicily. With thousands of casualties and having frequently visited the front lines himself, General Patton expressed great sympathy for his wounded soldiers and he frequently visited hospitals to support his men and to ensure that his wounded troops received proper care. Patton had no sympathy however for anyone hospitalized for stress, nerves or shell shock. Twice in August 1943, Patton slapped, kicked, threatened and abused soldiers who entered hospitals under the claim of stress, nerves or that they "can't take it anymore." Unable to contain himself, Patton used boundless profanity and physically assaulted such men, demanding their immediate return to the front lines. After the first incident on August 3, 1943, Patton recorded in his diary that the weeping soldier was an "arrant coward," that he "should be tried for cowardice and shot," and that "one sometimes slaps a baby to bring it to." Two days later, Patton issued a memo to his commanders explaining that "those who are not willing to fight will be tried by court-martial for cowardice in the face of the enemy."

During a second incident on August 10, 1943, a shivering artilleryman on a hospital cot told Patton "It's my nerves. I can't stand the shelling anymore." Believing there was no such thing as "combat fatigue" and that it was necessary to "put some fight back in him," Patton called the man a "goddamned coward," a "yellow son of a bitch," and a "disgrace to the army," further exclaiming that "you are going back to the front to fight." Pulling his pistol from its holster, Patton exclaimed "you ought to be lined up against a wall and shot. In fact, I ought to shoot you myself right now, God damn you!" Before leaving the hospital, Patton informed the doctors that "I won't have those cowardly bastards hanging around our hospitals. We'll probably have to shoot them some time anyway, or we'll raise a breed of morons." Patton later wrote in his diary that "I cursed him well and he shut up. I may have saved his soul if he had one."

These and other incidents led to an investigation that nearly ended Patton's military career. Recognizing however that "Patton is indispensable to the war effort" and that Patton himself was under tremendous combat stress, General Dwight Eisenhower instead issued Patton a strong letter of reprimand and a "severe bawling out." Patton later apologized to the men, but noted in his diary that "it is rather a commentary on justice when an Army commander has to soft-soap a skulker to placate the timidity of those above." Eisenhower removed Patton from command of the 7th Army and struggled over his ultimate fate. Although rejecting recommendations that Patton be relieved of WW II command, Eisenhower decided not to assign Patton command of an Army in Europe, electing instead to assign him command of the Third Army, which was still training in the United States. While Patton was disgruntled with being deprived of the opportunity to participate in the upcoming D-Day invasion of Normandy, he was fortunate nonetheless to have an Army command. Patton noted of the assignment: "Well, I have an Army and it is up to me. . . . As far as I can remember this is my twenty-seventh start from zero since entering the U.S. Army. Each time I have made a success of it, and this must be the biggest." The Third Army would eventually include TW and the 94th Infantry Division and would go on to fight under Patton's leadership in some of the bloodiest battles of WW II.

In November 1943, TW completed basic training and was sent by train to Gainesville, Florida. At the University of Florida, TW roomed with Gus Stavros and entered the ASTP (Army Specialized Training Program), where he studied engineering. The ASTP program provided education and specialized technical training to academically promising GIs who met eligibility criteria including education, age and intelligence, the latter of which required achieving at least a score of 110 on the Army General Classification Test.

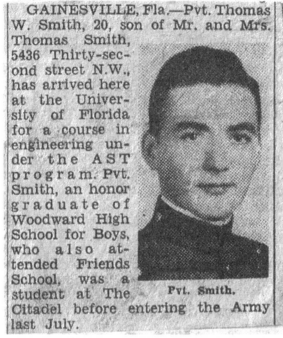

GAINESVILLE, Fla.—Pvt. Thomas W. Smith, 20, son of Mr. and Mrs. Thomas Smith, 5436 Thirty-second street N.W., has arrived here at the University of Florida for a course in engineering under the AST program. Pvt. Smith, an honor graduate of Woodward High School for Boys, who also attended Friends School, was a student at The Citadel before entering the Army last July.

Pvt. Smith.

Washington Star, December 18, 1943

TW "studying" engineering at the University of Florida

The ASTP program was intended to provide the Army with high-level technicians and specialists, although some families who had children die in combat thought the program was used by rich and influential families to shield their children from war.

From the University of Florida, TW sent his parents the postcard below with a postmark of December 15, 1943:

On the back of the postcard, TW wrote:

> *Dear Mother and Dad,*
>
> *Send me my Citadel physics book as soon as possible. They say they are cracking down. I want to be ready. Some of the subjects are on the sophomore level and are covered in three months. They are cramming everything down our throats. The physics book I want is blue. I am well and feeling fine.*
>
> *your son,*
> *Tom*

Despite occasional napping, TW studied hard and completed a course in basic engineering on March 4, 1944, for which he received the certificate below.

Army Specialized Training Program

The ARMY *of the* UNITED STATES *hereby certifies that*

PVT. THOMAS W. SMITH 14192063

has completed satisfactorily the course of study in

BASIC ENGINEERING

pursued at UNIVERSITY OF FLORIDA.

His training was completed on 4 MARCH 1944. *The record of his performance is available, on request by appropriate authority, for the purpose of determining his academic credit.*

BY ORDER OF THE SECRETARY OF WAR:

R. S. JOHNSON, FOR CERTIFYING INSTITUTION
Registrar

RALPH L. JOYNER, COMMANDANT
Lt. Colonel, F.A.

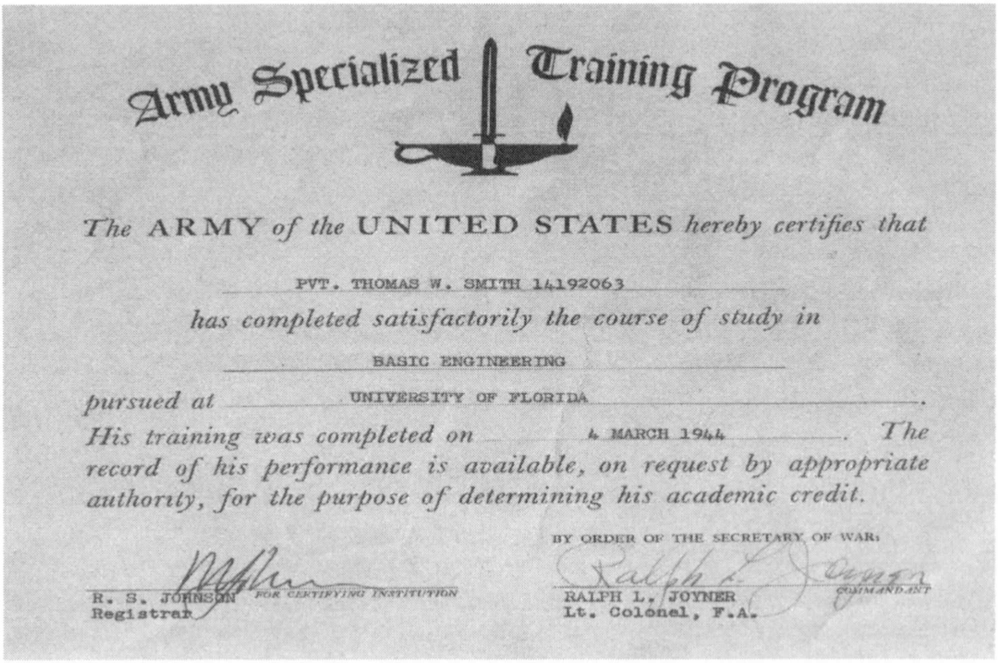

TW enjoyed his studies at the University of Florida, and noted *"that was a good deal but it terminated in March 1944,"* which explains why the back of the above certificate says "separated: convenience of the government." Several months earlier, in December 1943, U.S. President Roosevelt, British Prime Minister Churchill and Soviet Premier Stalin had agreed to invade France in June 1944. As a consequence, the ASTP program was cancelled because 134,000 infantry replacements were needed for the invasion of France. Ed Cowley, of the 94th Infantry Division's AT 301st Regiment, later recalled:

> We probably sensed that something wasn't right. And then we got the news. Our apprehensions were confirmed when the company was assembled and Captain Heron announced in solemn tones that the plans for us had changed—a decision had been made by the Secretary of War that we weren't needed in college as much as we were needed in the infantry. . . . About 2,000 of us 18-year olds were suddenly on our way to the infantry for real. So mothers, you may now keep your service flags right where you have them.

TW was then sent by troop train to Mississippi, where he and his buddies boarded trucks, stenciled with the number 94, headed to Camp McCain, in Grenada, Mississippi. One of several training sites created in Mississippi during World War II, Camp McCain was created in 1942 and named after Major-General Henry Pinckney McCain. Major-General McCain (1861-1941) is known as the father of the Selective Service and had been responsible for setting up the WW I draft that included Tom Sr. twenty-five years earlier. Henry McCain was also a distant uncle of Arizona Senator and 2008 Presidential candidate John S. McCain, III. In the Saga of the 94th Infantry Division, Camp McCain was described as a "rugged looking setup" and rumored to be the "hell hole of the U.S. Army." Camp McCain has also been described as the "home of the 94th Infantry Division." TW was assigned to the 94th Infantry Division at Camp McCain, and in a September 20, 1995, letter to another 94th Infantry Division veteran, TW noted:

> *When the program was disbanded in March 1944, I ended up as a rifleman (M-1) First Platoon, Company E, 301st Regiment, 94th Division, Camp McCain, Mississippi.*

Meanwhile in Europe, on March 24, 1944, 76 allied prisoners of war escaped from Stalag Luft III, a German Luftwaffe (Air Force) prisoner of war camp in Sagan, Poland, about 100 miles southeast of Berlin. Using some 4,000 bed boards, 90 beds, 62 tables, 34 chairs and 76 benches, the prisoners had constructed three elaborate tunnels which they named "Tom," "Dick" and "Harry." The Germans captured 73 of the escaped prisoners, 50 of whom were executed under orders from Hitler. Referred to as "The Great Escape," the story has been the subject of popular books, movies, songs and video games.

Quoting again from the Reverend Charles Manning, 94th Infantry Division, 301st Regiment, Company H, speaking at a 94th Division Association reunion in 1996:

> Few, if any, of us had any idea of the role that Almighty God had chosen for the 94th Infantry Division to play in World War II. The war was so big and bad and we were so small and naïve.

TW's friend and classmate David Bell was training in Muskogee, Oklahoma, and was assigned to the 42nd Infantry Rainbow Division in the Seventh Army. The Rainbow Division is the same division TW's father served in during WW I.

The 94th Infantry Division trained with live ammunition at Camp McCain, running combat exercises and infiltration courses laden with barbed wire while live charges were detonated and machine guns fired overhead. Such training inevitably led to tragic accidents, including two officers from the 376th Infantry Regiment who were killed during night training exercises. Despite stressful and trying conditions, TW recalls some good times during this period, and he made many close friends. In a January 28, 1995, letter to former ASTP roommate and fellow 94th Infantry Division veteran Gus Stavros, TW would ask:

> *Remember the Twin Diner in East Orange, N.J., Murphee Hall at the University of Florida, remember when your mother visited you at Camp McCain and took the two of us to the movies, as I recall it was a Danny Kaye movie.*

In a February 1989 letter to fellow 94th Infantry veteran Doug Benson, TW remembered another ASTP and Camp McCain buddy named Augustus "Gus" F. Allen, III, who shared KP duties with TW and was later killed in Germany:

> *In World War II army serial numbers of draftees started with a 3. Gus pointed out to me when we were on KP that neither his ASN nor mine started with a 3 (not sure but his may have been a 4; mine was a 1). He noted that most of the men in the E company were draftees and joked as to why we had to be KP's for all the "3's" draftees. It was his contention that they should be serving us.*

TW's serial number was 14192063. The first digit indicated that TW was one of the nearly six million enlisted soldiers in WW II, as opposed to the large majority of U.S. servicemen and women who were draftees. The Selective Service System in WW II drafted approximately sixteen million men and women, each of whom were given serial numbers that started with the number 3.

One of TW's closest friends from both the ASTP program and Camp McCain was Tom Leary, who had been a student at Texas A&M University before being drafted. TW remembers that Tom Leary was the same age as TW and that Leary was an *"all around good guy who was very easy to get along with."*

Thomas Ross Leary at Camp McCain, MS.

Tom Leary remained TW's *"best buddy"* in the early war years and the two men were together when Leary was killed during the Battle of the Bulge. In addition to Leary, TW recalls a number of ASTP friends who were assigned to the 94th Division at Camp Mc-Cain. TW spent many hours, days, weeks and months with these young men, both training and later fighting Germans. Under these circumstances and recognizing Benjamin Franklin's observation that "we must all hang together, or most assuredly we shall hang separately," TW became close friends with his fellow ASTP GIs, and in notes written decades later, TW remembered some of their names:

> *There were thirteen in my group of boys from ASTP who joined the 94th Division at Camp McCain in March 1944. We were all assigned as infantry riflemen. Six months later we were overseas and in combat. By war's end six of the group had been killed in action (KIA): Bernard Goodlevege, Samuel Harvey, Stanton Null, Al Kabic, Thomas Leary and Marshall Leigh. Four members of the group were wounded in action (WIA): Walter Meeks, William Pardue, Gus Stavros and Graham Northrup.*

In May 1944, the Under Secretary of War Robert Patterson informed the 94th Division at Camp McCain that they were the first "expert" infantry division, and TW later wrote with pride that *"I took part in a training exercise that earned the 94th the distinction of being the first Expert Infantry Division in the Unites States Army."*

TW, Pfc. Infantry Rifleman, Camp McCain, MS.

At Camp McCain, TW had one of the highest marksman points in his company and was designated a company sniper. TW's military qualifications papers after the war included "Expert, Rifle M1, Rifle, Enfield 1917."

In another letter, dated January 20, 1994, to a fellow FBI retiree, TW wrote:

> *At the time I held the most important position in the army—Pfc. Infantry Rifleman (Patton's Third Army). Many people were surprised as they thought I served in the Confederate Army.*

TW was assigned to the 94th Infantry Division's 301st Regiment, E Company, 1st Platoon, which later became part of General Patton's Third Army. The 301st Infantry Regiment was created during WW I, with a motto "From This Center Liberty Sprang."

By May 1944, the Germans occupied Rome, with Mussolini as the self-declared head of German-occupied northern Italy; the Allies had reached Messina, Sicily and Naples, Italy; and Soviet troops had advanced into Poland.

E-301 1st Platoon at Camp McCain, MS., March 1944 (TW standing 6th from the left)

E-301 1st Platoon at Camp McCain, MS., May 1944 (TW standing 4th from left)

TW's platoon, the 1st Platoon of E Company of the 301st Regiment, was commanded by Lieutenant Edmund G. Reuter, Jr. Lieutenant Reuter later wrote that the 1st platoon's radio call sign was "celebrate white," and that the 1st platoon was also referred to as "Easy One (the phonetic alphabet at that time—some years later changed to echo.)" Reuter noted that "on patrols and special operations, the 1st platoon was always called 'Root', an aberration of my last name" and that the 2nd platoon was called "Fish." TW remained in touch with Lieutenant Reuter long after the war until Reuter passed away in 2007. In a December 1, 1998 letter to Lieutenant Reuter, TW noted:

> As an officer you were the only leader I served under. You went with us on patrols, over hedge rows, thru mine fields, into forests with tree bursts over our heads and close in street fighting. Most of the other officers I only saw in rear echelon…. Let me emphatically state I am proud to have served in Lt. Reuter's 1st platoon.

TW and his fellow 1st platoon buddies respected Lieutenant Reuter, and the feeling was mutual. Years later, Lieutenant Reuter would write to Sergeant James Green's wife, Millie, noting his admiration for Sergeant Green and the E-301 1st platoon, explaining "with as fine a group of men as I have seen in three wars—not a buffoon in the bunch— all pulling together, we succeeded in accomplishing all of our missions."

Under General Patton's leadership, TW's chain of command in the 94th Infantry Division is noted below and included Lieutenant Colonel Donald Hardin, who was the uncle of Dave Bell's wife, Pat.

- General George Smith Patton, Jr. – 3rd Army
  - Major General Walton H. Walker – XX Corps
    - Major General Harry J. Malony – 94th Infantry Division
      - Colonel Roy N. Hagerty (Commander) – 301st Regiment
        - Lieutenant Colonel Donald Hardin (Exec. Officer) – 301st Regiment
          - Lieutenant Colonel Francis H. Dohs – 2nd Battalion
            - Captain Walter J. Stockstad – E Company
              - Lieutenant Edmund G. Reuter – 1st Platoon
                - Sergeant James W. Green – 1st Platoon, 3rd Squad
                  - Private TW Smith – 1st Platoon, 3rd Squad

In general, a squad of twelve men was led by a Sergeant; three squads and a weapons team made up a platoon, led by a Lieutenant; three platoons and headquarters personnel made up a company, led by a Captain; three companies and a headquarters company made up an approximately 800 man battalion, led by a Lieutenant Colonel; three battalions made up a regiment, led by a Colonel; three regiments made up a division, led by a Major General; two or more divisions made up an Army corps, led by a Major General.

Pictures of General Patton hanging in TW's office

In addition to TW's 301st Infantry Regiment, the 94th Infantry Division consisted of two other rifle regiments, the 302nd and the 376th infantry regiments, as well as supporting reconnaissance, artillery, medical, engineer combat, quartermaster, ordnance, signal and military police elements. Comprised of over 15,000 men, the 94th Infantry Division was one of twenty-five infantry divisions utilized in General George S. Patton, Jr.'s Third Army. Patton assigned the Third Army the code name "Lucky." At full strength, the Third Army included over 400,000 men. TW was part of the XX Corps, which was one of four Corps units under Patton. The XX Corps was commanded by Major General Walton H. Walker, who was later killed during the Korean War. Nicknamed "Bulldog" both for his build and demeanor, Walker was described as a Patton favorite, about whom Patton once noted "He will apparently fight anytime, anywhere, and with anything that I will give to him to fight."

Nicknamed "old blood and guts," General Patton was a widely decorated war veteran and a colorful, fearless and demanding leader. General Eisenhower once noted "It is no exaggeration to say that Patton's name struck terror at the hearts of the enemy." Patton lived and breathed military service, exclaiming that "compared to war, all other forms of human endeavor shrink to insignificance." Believing in "speed and vigor of action" and that "a pint of sweat will save a gallon of blood," Patton demanded spit and polish, as well as unconditional discipline, which he defined as "instant, cheerful, unhesitating obedience." TW's friend the Reverend Charles Manning, H-301, described Patton "as maniacal as a coach in a championship game; [he] screamed at your imperfections, screamed about your frozen feet, screamed about your number of casualties, screamed about those who had no choice but to surrender."

Upon being given command of the Third Army, General Patton summed up three reasons for the United States' involvement in WW II during his first address to his Third Army troops:

The first is because we are determined to preserve our traditional liberties. The second is to defeat and crush the Nazis, who would destroy our liberties. The third is because men like to fight and always will fight. . . . If you don't like to fight then I don't want you around here. You better get out now before I kick you out later.

Patton motivated his men with personal guarantees: "I can assure you that the Third United States Army will be the greatest army in American history." He reminded his troops "do not take counsel of your fears," while at the same time warning them that "some crazy German bastards" were trying to "rule the world" by "looting, killing, and abusing millions of innocent men, women and children" and that "we are fighting to defeat and wipe out the Nazis who started all this goddamned son-of-a-bitchery." After instilling in his men "an adequate hatred of Germans," Patton reminded his troops that "killing wins wars," that "no bastard ever won a war by dying for his country, they won by making the other dumb bastard die for *his* country," and that "if we go forward with desperation, if we go forward with utmost speed and fight, these people cannot stand against us." Patton demanded that his men "do ever in all things our damdest and never oh never retreat." He also demanded that his men "never surrender," preferring instead to "succeed or die in the attempt" and to leave the battlefield as "either a conqueror or a corpse." Patton's sentiments were shared earlier by General George Washington, who once ordered during the Revolutionary War that "if any man in action shall presume to skulk, hide himself, or retreat from the enemy, without the orders of his commanding officer, he will be instantly shot down, as an example of cowardice."

Let alone cowardice, Patton abhorred even the word defense, preferring instead to "always attack." As noted by fellow General O.P. Weyland:

Despite his colorful language, he had his own version of religion. Being a cavalryman, Patton believed in open warfare and in the old cavalry adage of "when in doubt, attack."

Patton's early field notes included his golden war rule of speed, simplicity and boldness and his belief that "War means fighting. Fighting means killing, not digging trenches. Find the enemy, attack him, invade his land, raise hell while you are at it." Patton acknowledged that "I have always talked blood and murder and am looked on as an advocate of close up fighting," and he consistently insisted that his men "attack. . . push forward, attack again until the end." Addressing his Third Army, Patton explained "I don't want to get any messages saying that 'we are holding our position.' We are not holding anything! . . . We are advancing constantly and we're not interested in holding on to anything except the enemy." During the Battle of the Bulge, Patton further explained that "The only way to win a war is to attack and keep on attacking, and after you have done that, keep attacking some more."

Years later, TW's platoon leader, Lieutenant Reuter, remembered one of General Patton's attack philosophies, to be implemented by TW and the rest of the 94th division troops in Germany:

> It was to be our first use of "marching fire," a new Patton philosophy which sounded like suicide (you were to start walking toward your objective until you encountered fire—then you opened up, firing at anything that was a likely target and just kept walking forward.)

Patton's use of marching fire was effective, as noted by Secretary of War Robert Patterson in an April 4, 1946, address at the dedication of Patton Hall at Fort Riley, Kansas:

> The introduction under combat conditions and training of the men in marching fire— infantry shooting from the shoulder or the hip as they advanced—developed the full effectiveness of the Garand rifle and made a company of foot soldiers the equivalent of a machine gun unit.

Patton was a tactical genius, always thinking of the campaign he was fighting, as well as the next campaign and the one after that. Patton was widely decorated, but appreciated that his medals were worn as a representative for his men who earned them. While he had no tolerance for "yellow cowards," whom he believed "should be killed off like flies," he stressed the importance of every man in the Army, from the ordnance staff supplying guns, the quartermaster bringing food and clothes, the cook in the mess hall, and the chaplain without whom "we would all go to hell."

Although TW and his friends joked that *"it was our blood and his guts,"* TW had great respect for General Patton and believed that Patton did not ask his men to do anything that he was not willing to do himself. Believing commanders must "lead in person," Patton spent a great deal of time on the front lines, causing one of his men to comment, "General, if you just move up there forty yards you will be in the enemy front lines." General Eisenhower similarly warned Patton that "I want you as a corps commander, not as a casualty." Nevertheless, Patton believed that the Army was like spaghetti: "You can't push a piece of spaghetti, you've got to pull it." Patton also empowered his men, believing that leaders must "never tell people how to do things; tell them what to do and they will surprise you with their ingenuity." The 94th Infantry Division was known as "Patton's Golden Nugget," and to this day, TW continues to note with pride that the middle initial "S" in General Patton's name stands for "Smith."

While TW and the 94th Infantry Division were completing their training and preparing to go to Europe, American troops were preparing for the June 6, 1944, invasion of Normandy, also known as D-Day, which is a military term for the beginning date of a military operation. On the eve of the Normandy invasion, General Patton spoke to Third Army troops already in England. With his customary straight talk and self-described "eloquent profanity," Patton exclaimed:

On June 6, 1944, nearly 160,000 Allied troops landed along a 50 mile stretch of coastline in Normandy, France, on beaches called Utah, Omaha, Gold, Juno and Sword. The complex and risky operation faced overwhelming forces, difficult terrain and the uncertainties of weather, and involved more than 5,000 ships and 13,000 Allied aircraft. Illustrating the risks and uncertainties of the operation, and the leadership and character of Supreme Allied Commander Dwight Eisenhower, who made the decision to launch the invasion, Eisenhower penciled the following note in his confidential files on June 5, 1944: "Our landings in the Cherbourg-Havre area have failed to gain a satisfactory foothold, and I have withdrawn the troops. My decision to attack at this time and place was based upon the best information available. The troops, the air and the navy did all that bravery and devotion to duty could do. If any blame or fault attaches to the attempt, it is mine alone." Fortunately, Eisenhower never needed this note and celebrated success instead. Although more than 9,000 Allied troops were killed or wounded during the D-Day invasion, the Allied Forces successfully secured a position in Normandy, from which they would begin the long march to defeat Hitler's Nazi forces in Europe.

Sure we want to go home. We want this war over with. The quickest way to get it over with is to go get the bastards who started it. The quicker they are whipped, the quicker we can go home. The shortest way home is through Berlin and Tokyo. And when we get to Berlin, I am personally going to shoot that paperhanging son-of-a-bitch Hitler. Just like I'd shoot a snake!

After the D-Day invasion, progress slowed considerably and criticism grew of the British ground commander Bernard Montgomery. While Patton's troops were readying for combat, Eisenhower grew impatient with progress in France, noting on June 27, 1944, "Sometimes I wish I had George Patton here." Characteristically anxious to join the fight, Patton believed that Montgomery preferred him on the sidelines, "as he fears I will steal the show, which I will."

On July 23, 1944, the entire 94th Infantry Division was transported in five trains to Camp Shanks, New York, located in the Catskill Mountains. TW recalls that at Camp Shanks, *we received more combat training, drills, inoculations, lectures and inspections.* Gas masks were distributed and the men were required to honor censorship orders to keep their location and destination secret. From Camp Shanks the division headed to New York City from where they departed for England on the Queen Elizabeth.

5. WEIGHING ANCHOR AND OFF TO ENGLAND

"Just for your records I will make another request for food so send me a box of food!"

In New York, over 15,000 men of the 94th Infantry Division, along with several thousand British personnel, loaded onto the Queen Elizabeth. The ship sailed across the Atlantic Ocean from New York to Greenock, Scotland, from August 6 to August 11, 1944.

TW recalls a crowded ride during which he bathed in salt water and shared a bunk with two other GIs who rotated from bunk to deck in three eight-hour shifts, referred to as triple bunking. An empty pool on the ship was used for food storage and as a mess hall, and TW recalls watching the same movie over and over with his fellow GIs to the point that they could recite practically every line.

Around the first of August we moved by rail to New York City where the whole division loaded aboard the luxury British liner Queen Elizabeth. On August 6th the Elizabeth weighed anchor. On the ship two meals were served every day and both were the same, "bully beef and tomatoes" with bread crumbs and cheese spread over them. Life jackets had to be worn at all times. We were not in convoy because no other ships could keep up with us. The ship zig zagged every three or four minutes. On several occasions however the ship changed course so abruptly that men were thrown from their bunks. They had learned that German subs were ahead and changed course. The first land we saw was Ireland as we entered the North Channel. Then we sailed up the Clyde to Greenock, Scotland, disembarked and went by train to Chippenham, England.

The SS Queen Elizabeth

A few days earlier, on August 4, 1944, Anne Frank and her family were arrested by the German Gestapo in Amsterdam, Holland, after two years of hiding. The Jewish family was sent to concentration camps where 15 year old Anne and her sister Margot later died of disease and her mother Edith died of starvation. Her father Otto survived and returned to Amsterdam, where he found Anne's diary, which was published in 1947. It has since been published in over 60 languages and is one of the most widely read books in the world.

This was TW's first trip outside of the United States and his first sight of the land of his ancestors, the Thompsons of England and the Steeles of Ireland and Scotland. Upon arriving later by train in Chippenham, TW recalls *"there we set up tents in an open field that had previously been bombed by the Germans."*

While in England, TW sent a letter to his parents, alluding to Germany's eventual defeat as a foregone conclusion and making a plea for food. GI letters were sent using v-mail, which was a photographed letter reduced to a 4" x 5" sheet for mailing. The postage was free and all letters included a censor's stamp at the top left corner to ensure that no confidential or sensitive information was communicated.

The reference in the letter to Prosise is Alan Brooke Prosise, who was one of TW's good friends from the Woodward School for Boys. Alan Prosise was a native Washingtonian who played football at the University of Virginia before heading off to World War II. He was later shot down, wounded and captured in Rhineland, Germany. Prosise is pictured with TW's parents on the far right in the adjacent picture.

The reference to Northrup is TW's friend Graham Northrup, who was also from Washington, D.C., and was TW's friend from the ASTP program. Northrup attended high school in Washington, D.C., with Dave Bell's future wife Pat. Northrup also was later wounded in Europe.

While in Chippenham, TW recalls his second "police" assignment.

While there I was assigned as an M.P. (military policeman) on a detail to nearby Bath England. I had to wear a blue arm band with white letters "M.P." around my left upper arm. My job was to walk around the town and see that the men from the 94th all behaved. A number of times Britishers came up to me and pointing to my M.P. arm band exclaimed "it's nice to have a Member of Parliament here in our town."

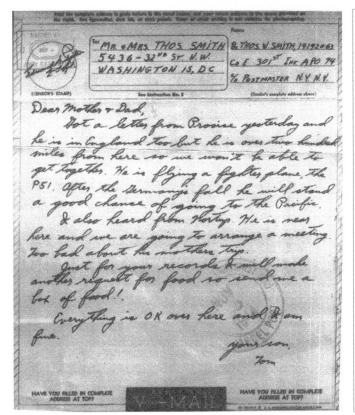

Dear Mother and Dad,

Got a letter from Prosise yesterday and he is in England too but he is over two hundred miles from here so we won't be able to get together. He is flying a fighter plane, the P51. After the Germany's fall he will stand a good chance of going to the Pacific.

I also heard from Northrup. He is near here and we are going to arrange a meeting. Too bad about his mothers trip.

Just for your records I will make another request for food so send me a box of food!

Everything is OK over here and I am fine.

> your son,
> Tom

On the evening of August 12, 1944, one day after TW landed in the United Kingdom, Lieutenant Joseph P. Kennedy, Jr., brother of future U.S. President John F. Kennedy, took off from an air base in London in a Navy plane loaded with 24,000 pounds of explosives. In response to German V-1 and V-2 rockets bombing London, the U.S. Army devised a plan to retaliate with B-17 and B-24 bombers packed with explosives and flown by remote radio control. Pilots were needed for take off, after which they would parachute over England once the plane leveled off. Their target was a German V-3 supergun weapon site in France. Colonel Elliott Roosevelt, President Roosevelt's son, piloted a plane following Kennedy. After Kennedy's plane was switched to radio-control, but before Kennedy and co-pilot Lieutenant Willford Willy ejected, the plane blew up over Blythburgh, England, killing both men. Colonel Roosevelt's plane was able to return home.

Itinerary TW saved of his taxi sightseeing tour of London

TW also recalls that *"while in England I was lucky enough to get a weekend pass to London. Saw all the sights including buzz bombs. I think they were called v-2's."* Above is the itinerary of TW's taxi sightseeing tour of London, arranged by the American Red Cross as a special tour for GIs. In addition to the standard sights, the tour included a visit to "Bombed Sites Around City of London," which was stop number 14 on the itinerary.

The fifth stop on the tour was Big Ben and the Houses of Parliament, where TW and three of his buddies posed for a picture. Although not yet attached to Patton's Third Army, TW and his 94th Infantry Division buddies were obediently well dressed and wore neckties, consistent with Patton's philosophy and mandate.

A short time later, around September 3, 1944, the 94th Infantry Division was transported to Southampton, England, from where they would depart for France.

94th Division Soldiers (left to right) Thomas F. Williams, Jr. (Ga.),
William H. Layton (Mo.), Peter P. SanFillipo (Il.), and TW (D.C.).

On August 31, 1944, Hitler informed his generals:
Under all circumstances we will continue this battle until, as Fredrick the Great said, one of our damned enemies gets too tired to fight any more. We'll fight until we get a peace which secures the life of the German nation for the next fifty or a hundred years and which, above all, does not besmirch our honor a second time, as happened in 1918. . . . I live only for the purpose of leading this fight. . . .

Hitler's Field Marshal Walter Model likewise demanded of his soldiers on the Western Front that "none of us gives up a square foot of German soil while still alive." By September 1944, the Allies had entered Germany and liberated Brussels, Antwerp, Cherbourg, and Paris. The Germans began a major counter-attack in Avranches and were fighting an uprising in Warsaw by the Polish Home Army, which would soon surrender to the Germans.

6. SANDY BEACHES IN FRANCE AND CHRISTMAS MEMORIES

"My company was the first one in the whole division to see action. Can't tell you anything about it, but the Germans came out second best."

Utah Beach

Following their stay in England, the 94th Division departed for Utah Beach in Normandy, France, on September 5-8, 1944. Under Colonel Hardin's command, TW's 301st Infantry Regiment boarded two Liberty ships and entered the English Channel on September 5, 1944. Liberty ships generally were uncomfortable and carried approximately 500 troops travelling under conditions that the Army acknowledged "lowered morale." TW's ship, named the Neutralia, landed on Utah beach on September 6.

> *We sailed past Cherbourg and heard explosions and could see flames and smoke in the distance. As we approached Utah Beach we could see all kinds of debris and even some bodies in the water. There was desolation and destruction everywhere. The Liberty Ship stopped and we had to climb over the rail down a cargo net to a smaller boat which took us ashore. Utah Beach was full of debris and we were told that some of the German camouflaged pillboxes [concrete forts] were still occupied. There was still a lot of barbed wire and occasionally a sign that said "Achtung Minen" [attention mines] with a picture of a skull and crossbones.*

Remembering the unlucky soldiers he saw floating in the ocean, TW notes *"it was the first time I'd seen a corpse outside of a coffin."* TW soon saw many more corpses. After arriving on Utah Beach, TW later observed German POW's picking up dead American GIs.

The Army's History of the 94th Infantry Division, published in 1948 and hereinafter referred to as the Division History, described the scene as follows:

> The waters off Utah Beach presented a scene of desolation and destruction as the 94th began debarkation. Visible were the wrecks of more landing craft and Liberty ships than a man would care to count. Masts, funnels, bows and sterns were thrust up from the waves at all manner of grotesque angles. . . . Dug into the dunes behind the beach and heavily camouflaged were the pillboxes, gun emplacements, firing pits, communication trenches, dugouts and shelters that had formed the German beach defenses. Long-barreled 88s [88 mm German anti-aircraft and anti-tank guns] still protruded from their firing apertures.

The majority of the 94th Infantry Division landed on Utah Beach on September 8, 1944, coincidentally exactly 94 days after D-Day. TW recalls that a German radio broadcaster known as "Axis Sally" reported that the 94th Division had arrived on the coast of France, and that the German Elph (11th) Panzer *was planning a suitable reception.* This was a sobering thought, and TW recalls that *"it was an unhealthy place."* One week earlier, Hitler issued orders that "all fighting bunkers of the West wall are to be defended by the crew until the last breath," adding further that "withdrawal is out of the question."

One of the first assignments for TW's platoon was to unload thousands of GI duffel bags, which Lieutenant Reuter later recalled as follows:

> Initially, just after arriving ashore at Utah Beach, LTC Dohs (2nd Battalion) personally selected me to go on a "Division baggage detail." We went back to this storage area and trucks came all that day, all that night and well into the following day. I never saw so many duffel bags—we should have had a company or battalion instead of one platoon . . . some 15,000 or so duffel bags. We started stacking them neatly, but ended leaving them wherever they were thrown off the trucks…. By morning I had men literally passed out from fatigue.

Following baggage detail, TW recalls that his regiment *"turned right"* and advanced into Brittany toward the ports of Lorient and St. Nazaire. Lieutenant Reuter remembered the trip to Brittany:

> LTC Hardin was surprised and happy to see me—he promptly put me in a jeep with driver and told me to lead the last half of the regiment forward (actually regimental trains). We were at Utah Beach and had to go to the Lorient-St. Nazaire area. . . a good distance. All along the way, there were French people

94ᵗʰ Division troops digging foxholes

lining the roads, waving and cheering, the girls throwing flowers; people giving us bottles of wine—reaching out to touch us, etc.

Upon reaching Lorient, TW recalled the division's assignment:

We then went to the general area of Lorient where we relieved the 6ᵗʰ armored division, a unit that had been badly decimated. Lorient on the channel coast of Brittany was the location of a German submarine base. They had constructed huge bunkers. The submarines would come in submerged, enter the bunkers and prepare for future raids on Atlantic shipping. Artillery protected the base from all sides.

In Brittany, the Army was said to occupy the longest line in its history, over 400 miles. The 94th Division got behind the Germans and cut off all ground support, so the Germans would have to rely on planes or submarines. As reported in the Army Times Combat Division summary:

In Lorient and St. Nazaire were 60,000 Nazis and first action of the 94ᵗʰ in September 1944 was the investment of these submarine ports, which were well protected by flak guns and concrete emplacements. The 94ᵗʰ covered 450 (airline) miles of front and the two pockets were effectively prevented from joining or breaking out.

Upon arriving in Brittany, TW's regiment dug foxholes, where they often slept and spent their time holding up the Germans and engaging in "frequent battles on the perimeter." Lieutenant Reuter recalled that:

The 1ˢᵗ platoon went on its combat and recon patrols out front, set up night ambushes out front (including the infamous French chicken patrol) and did everything anyone else did and lost no one—until Orscholz.

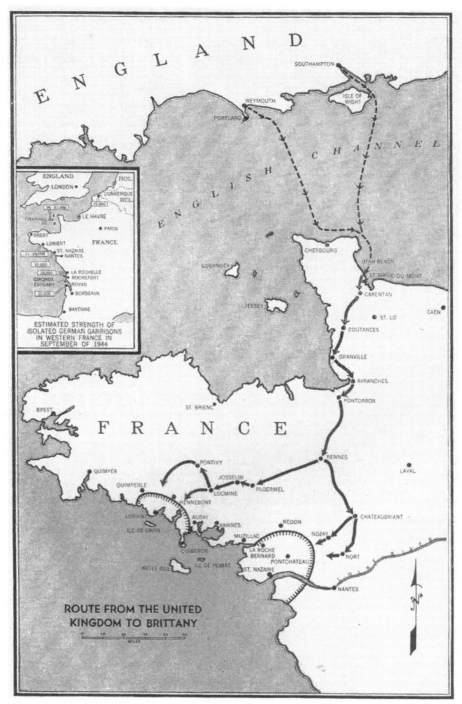

Source: History of the 94th Infantry Division

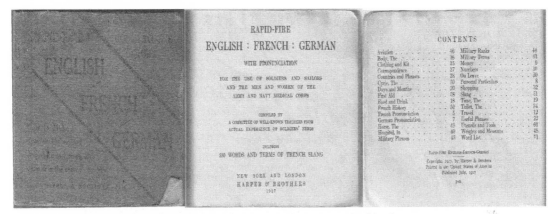

TW's translation book: cover, inside cover, and table of contents

At one point during this period, TW recalls walking near enemy territory.

> *I saw a French man and asked what all the loud noises were. The French man responded "Allemands," so I asked "Beaucoup Allemands?" The French man answered "Tres beaucoup Allemands." I replied, "au revoir."*

To communicate with French and German citizens, TW carried a small translation book, entitled *Rapid-fire English/French/German, How to Make Yourself Understood Anywhere in France, Belgium or in the Enemy's Country, For the Soldier Going to the Front.* The translation book is copyrighted 1917 and contains phrases TW and his fellow GIs commonly used, such as:

Have you seen any Germans?
> French: Avez-vous vu des Allemands?
> German: Haben Sie Deutsche gesehen?

Halt! Who Goes There?
> French: Halte! Qui vive?
> German: Halt! Wer da?

Help me to dig a trench.
> French: Aidez-moi a creuser une tranchée
> German: Helfen Si emir mit einem Laufgraben

Referring to the 94th Infantry Division, the French sometimes used the two digits nine and four, which in French translate to neuf and quatre. The pronunciation sometimes sounded like "neuf cat," which some used as a nickname for the 94th Infantry Division.

TW (middle) and GIs in France or Germany

During their three and a half month stay in Brittany, the 94th division liberated Blain (located near Nozay) and prepared and equipped 29 French battalions for battle. Although he always spoke highly of his British counterparts, TW and his fellow GIs were less complementary of the French, who were often untrained and lacked discipline:

The French soldiers were always willing to fight . . . . Right behind us.

The main thing the French did was go into the houses and steal stuff.

Sometimes we'd turn over German prisoners to the French. They were often cruel to them.

The experience of two other 301st Regiment GIs who came under fire during this period in Brittany was of similar sentiment and was later described by a nephew, Eddie Maul. Maul wrote "unfortunately there was no badge or pay raise; the next day the Captain told them that it did not count because it was not the enemy shooting at them, but their allies, the Free French."

In addition to his translation book, TW carried an infantry rifle with a bayonet, an ammunition belt, and a knapsack with sleeping bag, trench tools, grenades, and other provisions, including a helmet that TW also used as a washbasin, bucket, shovel or seat. TW recalls one of his early assignments was to guard a tunnel with another GI. The two men were told by a high ranking officer that no one was to enter or exit the tunnel under any circumstance. When a lower ranking officer approached and told TW and the other GI to move out of the way, TW and his fellow private refused. When the officer persisted, TW recalls *"my buddy said 'step aside TW so I don't get any blood on you when I carry out our orders with this M-1 rifle.' The officer turned around and left. We did not hear from him again."*

Recalling some of the early action years later, TW remembers that his regiment was the first regiment in the 94th Infantry division to see combat, and one of the first GIs killed in the 94th division was TW's friend Marshall Tyler Leigh. Marshall Leigh had attended Amherst College and was from Memphis, Tennessee. Marshall was in the ASTP program at Old Miss and, like TW, was assigned to E-301 at Camp McCain. Writing of Marshall's death to fellow WW II veteran Brad Newsom on June 29, 1994, TW wrote,

> *I think Marshal was among the first 94th boys killed in action. We had just pulled up on the line around 9/8/44 near Lorient, France. At dawn the following day, without warning, we were hit by an eighty-man German combat patrol. Marshal and three others were killed, several wounded and at least one boy from E-301 was captured by the Germans. We likewise killed, wounded and captured several Germans. Learned they were Kriegsmarines from the submarine base of Lorient. They had been told there was a new American unit on the line and their orders were not to return without an American prisoner.*

Marshall Leigh, Morris Faulkner, Glenn Loper and Omar McQueen of Company E, and L.B. Brandt of Company F, were the first battle casualties of the 301st Regiment. They were killed on September 11, 1944, when two German combat patrols of over 100 men attacked 94th Division combat posts at dawn. The Army's History of the 94th Infantry Division reported that the Germans attempted to burn two of the bodies in a haystack, but E-301 troops recovered the bodies before they could be destroyed.

Following WW I, General Patton wrote to General Pershing explaining that "the noise of the shells and the machine guns made me feel very homesick. War is the only place where a man truly lives." Perhaps sharing that sense of homesickness and exhilaration, TW wrote to his mother and father (right) on September 26, 1944. This time he noted with excitement that his was the first company in the *"whole division"* to see action, which would increase his pay by $5 a month. In 1944, the base pay for a Private First Class was $40 per month. While the new combat veteran could not provide battle details due to communication censors, TW did note that *"the Germans came out second best"* and that his parents were not to worry because he was *"getting along just fine."*

September 26, 1944

Dear Mother and Dad,

Now I will be getting five dollars a month more combat pay. My company was the first one in the whole division to see action. Can't tell you anything about it but the Germans came out second best. Guess that makes me a full fledged veteran.

My company did not have pictures made like Hopper's. However, while I was in London I had my picture made standing in front of Big Ben and the House of Parliament. The picture is in my barracks bag now and I can't get to it. When I get a chance I'll send you the picture.

There is no other news for now. Don't worry about me, I am getting along just fine. As yet none of the boxes have arrived.

your son,
Tom

TW's excitement was perhaps reminiscent of a young George Washington who in 1753 noted after a conflict with Indian and French troops that "I heard the bullets whistle; and believe me there is something charming in the sound." Sharing similar sentiments following the end of WW I, Winston Churchill exclaimed that "nothing in life is so exhilarating as to be shot at without result," and Captain Harry S. Truman concluded that despite its many horrors, the war was "the most terrific experience of my life."

The reference to Hopper is TW's childhood friend from Washington, D.C., Thomas Hopper. While TW was still thinking about "boxes" of food in France, back in the states, Janet Smith, nee Meyer, whom TW met and married after the war, recalls closely following WW II events from her small hometown of Melrose, Minnesota.

> We did not have TV then, so we listened to the radio constantly for news about the war. I remember everyone missing and being concerned about the boys in service, and there was great sadness in this small community whenever anyone was injured, missing or killed in action. My mother prepared care packages for my brother who was in the army. As I recall she would send cookies and candy and toiletries, I believe, and whatever else was allowed or requested.

I remember well the food rationing and use of stamps to get sugar and meat. Nylon stockings were also very scarce, and I remember women using a colored lotion on their legs to look like stockings, and drawing a line up the back to look like a seam, as all nylon stockings in that period had a seam up the back.

Janet's experience was shared by many Americans on the home-front, where home gardens were grown, gas and food were rationed, and resources were recycled and conserved for war production to ensure that "the boys" had weapons, ammunition and food. As another means of conserving resources, President Roosevelt instituted year round daylight savings time from 1942 to 1945. Using concepts suggested over a century earlier by Benjamin Franklin, daylight savings time was first observed in the United States in 1918 during WW I, following the earlier lead of Germany, Austria and many other countries seeking to conserve energy for the war. By the time of TW's letter, America's factories were producing one new warplane every five minutes and three new liberty ships every day. With dedicated resources to the war effort, the country would build 1,200 new warships in less than four years.

Later during the winter of 1944 as the holidays approached, TW remembers that while in position in France, a single engine plane came from the far right, flew overhead and dropped a large object.

> *A single engine German plane flew in from the east and dropped a large object which we concluded was a bomb. We all hit the dirt. After the plane left and there was no explosion it was discovered that the object dropped was a bag of mail for the Germans in the Lorient area. It contained wrapped candy, cheese and Christmas cards.*

TW recalls that some of the GIs ate the German candy. Never one to trust a German, TW declined. During most of the war, TW ate C-rations and K-rations, which were individually packaged daily food rations containing items such as canned meat or cheese products, biscuits, bouillon powder, chewing gum, powdered coffee, cigarettes and toilet paper. TW did not smoke cigarettes, but recalls that they came in handy nonetheless.

> *I traded the cigarettes with other GIs for food.*

Cigarettes also came in handy for TW's friend Harold A. Kane, who served with TW in Company E, 301st Regiment. Kane relayed his own experience with cigarettes in a 1989 94th Division Commemorative History:

> Sitting at my machine gun emplacement, I had just started to light my cigarette with my wick type lighter. I dropped it. I leaned over to retrieve the lighter and a shell burst right in front of my position. It split a tree located about a foot behind me, exactly where my head had been a moment before. Guess you could say I am one of the few whom smoking has saved.

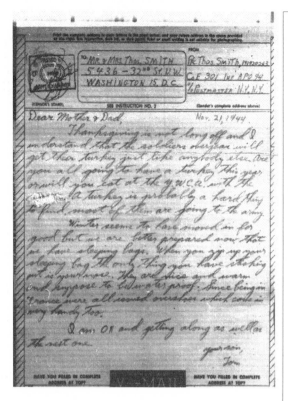

PFC. Thos. Smith
14192063
Co. E 301 Inf APO 94
%Postmaster NY, NY
November 21, 1944

Dear Mother and Dad,

Thanksgiving is not long off and I understand that the soldiers overseas will get their turkey just like anybody else. Are you all going to have a turkey this year or will you eat at the YWCA with the neighbors. A turkey is probably a hard thing to find, most of them are going to the army.

Winter seems to have moved in for good but we are better prepared now that we have sleeping bags. When you zip up your sleeping bag the only thing you have sticking out is your nose. They are nice and warm and supposed to be water proof. Since being in France we're all issued overshoes which come in very handy too.

I am OK and getting along as well as the next one.

your son,
Tom

Just before Thanksgiving on November 21, 1944, TW wrote home a third time. Again referencing food, TW anticipated that he and his fellow GIs would get turkey for Thanksgiving. Noting that *"winter seems to have moved in for good,"* he also mentioned the sleeping bags and overshoes issued by the army in response to cold weather conditions. TW would later find that the cold weather shoes issued by the Army were not as warm, waterproof and "handy" as he originally anticipated.

Following this third letter to his parents, the fighting would soon intensify and TW did not write home again until after the Battle of the Bulge. TW believes the following picture was taken of his E-301 first platoon not long before subsequent fighting where most of the original platoon were later killed, wounded or imprisoned.

During the fighting in Lorient and St. Nazaire, the 94th division captured 566 German prisoners, and the Germans captured 140 Allied soldiers, including GIs of the 301st regiment patrols. TW recalls seeing the capture of ten American airmen in Lorient. On

TW is sitting in the front row, third from the right. TW believes that he is the only member of the original E-301 1st Platoon still alive today.

December 18, 1944, a B-17 bomber crew returning from a mission in Regensburg was hit by enemy flak and lost all radio communication. Nearly out of fuel, the crew landed the plane in a field at Lorient, only to realize they were in enemy territory where they were immediately surrounded by German soldiers with weapons drawn. Following the capture and removal of the crew, 94th Division artillery observers destroyed the plane. These prisoners were later returned to the 94th Division on December 28 in the third of three prisoner exchanges negotiated on a "rank for rank" basis.

During this period, General Patton discovered instances where Allied prisoners in German camps were suffering from illness and malnutrition. Upon learning during an inspection that German prisoners in American camps were being fed more than American soldiers, Patton ordered the commanding officer to personally weigh each prisoner food ration and not to provide a fraction of an ounce more than required by international treaty. In contrast to Patton's efforts to abide by the rules, Hitler ingrained his own philosophy in his generals: "The victor will not be asked afterwards whether he told the

History of the 94th Infantry Division photo of 94th Infantry Division prisoner exchange, which included the explanation "Krauts going in. . .GIs coming out, at the St. Nazaire exchange."

truth or not. When starting and waging a war it is not right that matters, but victory"; and "whether right or wrong, we must win. . . and when we have won, who will ask us about the method?"

As Christmas approached in 1944, General Patton offered a Christmas greeting and prayer:

> Grant us fair weather for Battle. Graciously hearken to us as soldiers who call upon Thee that armed with Thy power, we may advance from victory to victory, and crush the oppression and wickedness of our enemies, and establish Thy justice among men and nations. Amen.

On Christmas Eve, some of the men of the L Company, 301st Regiment, attended a Catholic Church service in Hennebont, which is in the Lorient area of France. To their surprise, a group of German soldiers entered the Church, following the Americans' lead of stacking their rifles and helmets at the door. Sitting in opposite pews during Christmas Eve mass, the two groups of men prayed together in the same church. As TW would learn the next day, however, this was a brief reprieve.

TW and his fellow GIs celebrated Christmas Day by being allowed to leave their foxholes one at a time to get Christmas dinner. This would be one of the GIs rare chances for a hot meal, instead of the usual K-rations and C-rations. TW recalls his excitement over his Christmas meal, which unfortunately was short-lived.

> *On Christmas Day 1944, we were told one at a time we should take our mess kit back behind the line where we would be given hot food. We must return to our fox hole and eat there. When it came my time I took my mess kit, went back and got a mess kit full of meat, potatoes, fruit. It was a real treat after the K-rations we had been living on. On the way back holding the mess kit with my rifle slung over my shoulder I heard a shot.*

Something fell in my mess kit. The shot hit a tree near me and some wood chips fell on my food. There was a second shot and the bullet went through the sleeve of my jacket just above my left wrist. It burned my jacket and long john underwear but didn't harm me. It did spoil my Christmas dinner and I went back to my fox hole and returned fire.

TW recalls that the shot on Christmas Day caused him to drop his mess kit on the ground, with the result that he missed his only chance for a hot meal that day. Nonetheless, he was thankful for escaping with only a hole in his coat.

On another day, TW recalls leaving his overcoat in a tree when he was down in a foxhole and the *"Germans nearly shot it to pieces."* TW also remembers that *"during the Christmas season at night we could hear the Germans playing Silent Night or 'Stille Nacht.'"* Unfortunately, this warm memory was short-lived, as TW notes *"I also remember being woken up at 2:00 am by the sound of German Panzers [tanks]."*

TW recalls other events occurring during the Christmas season that would lead to a new assignment for the 94th Division:

The 66th Infantry Division started across the English Channel on Christmas Eve 1944. One of the transports, the Leopoldville, which was carrying two infantry regiments, was torpedoed by a German submarine. Almost 800 men were killed in the action. The Battle of the Bulge had started. Because of the Battle of the Bulge and the losses of the 66th Infantry Division, it was decided that the 66th should replace the 94th Division with the additional help of units from the French Forces of the Interior (FFI).

With the arrival of the remaining 66th Infantry Division and the FFI, TW and the 94th Infantry Division moved out of Brittany France on New Year's Day, 1945. The 94th Division had inflicted 2,700 German casualties while containing the German troops in Lorient and St. Nazaire, and was moving on to fight against Adolf Hitler's aggressive Ardennes Offensive, also known as the Battle of the Bulge.

By December 1944, the Allies captured Aachen, Germany, a civil war erupted in Greece, the U.S. began bombing mainland Japan, and the German Waffen SS murdered 81 U.S. prisoners of war at Malmedy, Belgium, during the opening days of the Battle of the Bulge. On December 28, 1944, Hitler demanded that his generals fight "with all your fire," and further exclaimed that "we shall then . . . smash the Americans completely. . . I do not believe in the long run the enemy will be able to resist forty-five German divisions."

7. ON TO GERMANY AND THE BATTLE OF THE BULGE

"Suddenly, Bang, Boom, Bang, German artillery was firing on us with tree bursts. Everybody was down, many were screaming from their wounds."

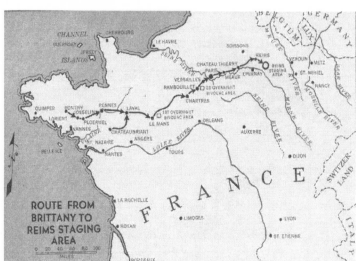

94th GIs boarding boxcars, and map of route to Battle of the Bulge.
Source: History of the 94th Infantry Division

TW remembers that *"additional troops were desperately needed on the Western Front and we went by 40x8s [40 men or 8 horses] box cars to the Ardennes offensive under General George S. Patton."* As TW moved out on New Year's Day, General Patton issued a New Year's message to his troops, noting "my New Year wish and sure conviction for you is that . . . you will continue your victorious course to the end that tyranny and vice shall be eliminated, our dead comrades avenged, and peace restored to a war-weary world." TW and his regiment traveled to Germany, first by box cars and then by truck and by foot. During the multi-day trip, TW remembers stopping only for fuel or provisions, creating logistical issues associated with sleep and bathroom relief out a boxcar door. Lieutenant Colonel

George Whitman of the 376th Infantry Regiment remembered that "these cars had no light except by opening sliding doors which allowed freezing blasts of air in—much to our discomfort." Along the way, TW saw Paris and passed Château-Thierry, Meaux and later St. Mihiel in France, where twenty-five years earlier, Tom Sr., Harry Truman and George Patton fought against Adolf Hitler and the German army in WW I.

At Reims, TW's regiment proceeded by truck through Metz and on to the front lines. The division traveled under difficult conditions, including "numbing January cold, icy winds, rain and finally snow," as reported in the History of the 94th Infantry Division:

> There were temporary delays as trucks skidded and ditched on the icy roads, and when exhausted drivers fell asleep at the wheel and lost control. In the unheated organics and troop carriers, the men suffered horribly from the cold. The steel truck floors literally sucked the warmth out of a man's feet and woolen gloves proved inadequate in temperatures only a few degrees above zero. Cases of frostbite were numerous, but unavoidable.

Upon arrival, the Division History noted that "guides were waiting and the half-frozen men of the 301st were led into the lines." TW later recalled:

> *We became involved in the attack of the Siegfried Switch Line which was the southern flank of the Bulge. It was a very important area because two major rivers converged there, the Saar River and the Moselle. These rivers formed the sides of a huge triangle whose apex was Trier, Germany. There were minefields everywhere. It was the coldest winter in Europe in 30 years and over twelve inches of snow on the ground. From then on we were involved in infantry fighting in woods, open fields and street fighting in small towns. For the most part, our main opponent was the German 11th Panzer Division, nicknamed the "Gespenster" (Ghost) Division, which was one of Germany's finest units on the Western Front.*

Named after a bulge created in the Allied Forces front lines, the Battle of the Bulge lasted from the middle of December 1944 to the end of January 1945. Hitler's initiative, which he thought would ultimately sever the United States alliance with Britain, successfully punched a bulge in the front line. While the battle caused more U.S casualties than any other during WW II, the Allied front was not penetrated and the Allies eventually retook the ground earlier lost and charged forward leading to Germany's eventual defeat.

Patton's Third Army fought on the southern boundary of the bulge and TW and the 94th Infantry Division initially fought in an area known as the Siegfried "switch line," also called the Saar-Moselle Triangle. The Siegfried Line extended some 390 miles along Germany's western border and contained thousands of tank traps and bunkers, which Hitler described as "impenetrable", "impregnable" and "invulnerable." The Siegfried "switch line" was a heavily fortified German position covering twelve miles of forested terrain, protecting railroad and communications facilities at Germany's oldest city of Trier. The area was protected by German antitank ditches, dragon's teeth (pyramid shaped concrete block-aids), pillboxes (concrete forts), bunkers and an extensive network of mines. In November 1944, while TW was in France, two Army divisions abandoned efforts to breach the switch line following heavy losses. In January 1945, the 94th Division was involved in multiple battles to stop the bulge, with a number of towns changing hands following attacks and counter-attacks that resulted in the loss of most of two of the Division's Companies.

TW understands that his E-301st Regiment had the unfortunate distinction of being the first 94th Division unit to suffer combat fatalities several months earlier, and by January 1945, the 94th Division sustained the largest number of casualties of any division in General Patton's Third Army. On January 14, 1945, the 94th Division "captured Tettingien and Butzdorf and three days later grabbed

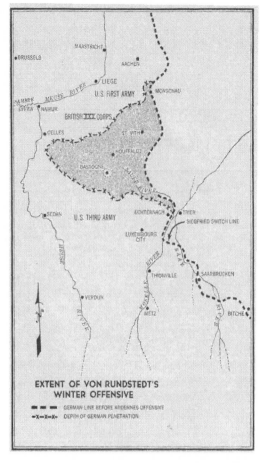

EXTENT OF VON RUNDSTEDT'S
WINTER OFFENSIVE
▬ ▬ ▬ GERMAN LINE BEFORE ARDENNES OFFENSIVE
–X–X–X– DEPTH OF GERMAN PENETRATION

Nennig, Wies and Berg, breaching the Switch line," as shown on a map of the Battle of the Bulge (opposite page). As the 94th division advanced, it also laid heavy minefields and affixed demolitions to bridges in the event the Germans should break through the line. With aggressive fighting, the division's chief of staff complained about the amount of ammunition that the division was using. Not to be deterred, however, General Patton authorized an increase in attack size, and the Division was later told to "shoot the works."

In a January 18, 1945, phone call, Major General Walton H. Walker, XX Corps Commander, explained to Major General Harry J. Malony, 94th Division Commander:

> *Walker*: Just had a call from Georgie. [Patton]. He said, "I understand you are in full retreat." He was kidding of course. You're going hard, are you?
>
> *Malony*: Hell Yes.

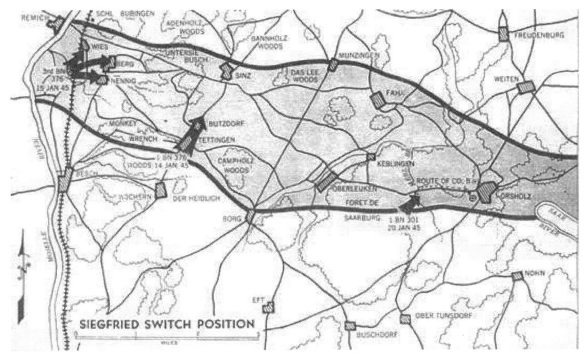

Source: History of the 94th Infantry Division

TW and his fellow veterans are not always clear on the exact timing and location of events during World War II. Soon after departing Lorient and St. Nazaire, Lieutenant Reuter recalled the 1st platoon's temporary stay in Launsdorf, France:

> The 1st Platoon, Easy, was billeted in a two story home with three French peasants, an old man, an old woman and a teen-age girl. They wore the wooden, straw-filled shoes that we found the norm back in Normandy and Brittany and black clothing, the woman covered in black formless dresses from chin to floor. We had several rooms and the French occupants had theirs. We slept on the floor in sleeping bags, about a dozen to a room.

Lieutenant Reuter further remembered:

> This was a rather pleasant stay—we were living inside and we weren't being endlessly shot at.

Following their stay at Launsdorf, TW's platoon moved out for an attack on Orscholz, Germany. After the 94th Division's capture of Nennig on Germany's right flank, which would later change hands again, General Malony's plan was to attack the left flank at

Orscholz. The town of Orscholz was located on a hill which, on the side assigned to TW's platoon, was surrounded by woods that were heavily fortified with "pillboxes, bunkers and communication trenches in the forest," and "felled trees to form a massive network of criss-crossing logs above and around them." Writing of the 94th Infantry Division, author Nathan Prefer noted that Orscholz was "the most fiercely defended position in the Siegfried Switch Line," and in contrast to the American infantry division, was supported by the 11th Panzer Division German armored unit. American GIs had not penetrated into the woods surrounding Orscholz, and to avoid detection, no patrols were sent until two days prior to the attack, which the 94th Division History described as follows:

> Then, a small carefully selected group was dispatched with instructions to proceed through the woods, to the rear of Orscholz, to determine the approximate strength of the enemy garrison. This patrol slipped into the deep forest and was never seen again.

The History of the 94th Infantry Division noted that "the weather was bitter cold and snow, already a foot deep on the ground, was descending so thickly it was hard to distinguish familiar landmarks." Perhaps as a result of the severe weather conditions, Lieutenant Reuter later wrote:

> I still have no idea exactly where we were relative to Orscholz and switch line fortifications.

The History of the 94th Infantry Division described TW's battalion's involvement in the beginning of the attack:

> On the morning of the 20th with the beginning of the first attack against Orscholz, the 2d Battalion, 301st, on the left of the regiment, had swung its right flank north, through the woods, in the direction of the attack. This action prevented the enemy from sending any forces from Oberleuken to counterattack the 1st Battalion.

In a March 7, 1999 letter to Doug Benson of E-301, TW wrote:

> *As I recall it in the latter part of January, E Company was in a little town named Landorf [Launsdorf, France]. I didn't know what country it was in, France or Germany, the people spoke both German and French. Around January 21st we formed a skimish line and moved out of town through a woods towards gunfire and pillboxes. There was snow everywhere and the weather was below freezing. As we were advancing suddenly there was artillery fire. Most of the shots hit the trees above our heads. With tree bursts there was no place to seek cover. As I recall, a number of men were wounded and two boys were killed on the spot. They both were ASTP boys, infantry riflemen Thomas Leary who was from Laredo, Texas, and Bernard Goodlevege, from Wilmington, Delaware.*

Writing years later, Lieutenant Reuter would write about this encounter:

> I had placed the first squad (positions had already been dug by some unit and it was getting dark) when a big gun in the distance fired (you could barely hear it go off and I always thought it was a railroad gun). It landed in our vicinity with a screaming approach and terrific crash. Obviously, someone was watching us and I speeded up the process of placement so we could all get under cover and to keep the gun from being able to zero in. However, it followed us right along— a second round landing just behind us. I had everyone placed but the last half of Green's 3rd squad and my headquarters group. When a third round fired in the distance—silence, then this screaming freight train crashed right into the midst of this last group of fast-moving men (about 10 people— Green's 6 [which included TW], me, Collins, Harvey and Simon). It landed on the edge of one of the holes we were moving into. By this time, it was dark. Goodlevege was killed instantly. In the dark, there didn't seem to be a mark on him. I was later told that a sliver of fragment went in behind his ear, leaving hardly any trace. He was my first loss…. Leary's left arm was blown off at the shoulder although he didn't know it. There wasn't enough left to put a tourniquet on. Several more rounds landed in the general area.

TW was with Tom Leary when Leary was hit, and TW recalled other details in a June 27, 1994, letter to fellow veteran Brad Newsom:

> *It was bitter cold with at least 12 inches of snow on the ground. Worst European winter in 30 years. After a scrap with the Germans we were advancing through a wooded area. It was dark. Suddenly "BANG, BOOM, BANG", German artillery was firing on us with tree bursts. Everybody was down, many were screaming from their wounds. I crawled up to Leary. He was on his back holding his chest and bleeding all over his left side. All he said was "I'm cold" and never another word or movement. I got the medic but he said "He's gone." Then I went over to Buckley. He was badly wounded in the leg but was sitting up and had already taken his wound tablet. I helped him apply a tourniquet. Later medics carried him and others out. They left Leary and three or four others who were dead.*

A few months later, fellow E-301 veteran Jim Mueller would write about the incident in a May 1945 letter:

> Tom Buckley had his leg broke by an 88. That shell got Goodlevege and hit Hammik and a couple others, but I cannot recall just who. Howells got a slug in his arm and ran around and told everyone that he had a million dollar wound.

TW remembered that Tom Buckley was from Milwaukee and was also from the ASTP program. Buckley was badly wounded that day, and TW notes that he *"never returned to E-301."*

Writing further about the incident, Lieutenant Reuter recalled:

> Meanwhile, my medic flipped out and was useless. Even so, there would not have been much he or anyone else could do…. I stayed with Leary and he asked me "Lieutenant, am I going to die?" He also asked "am I hurt bad?" I assured him he wasn't and explained that Sergeant Collins had gone for a stretcher party and he'd be out of there shortly, to just relax, and not worry, knowing there was a 99% chance I was lying to him. It was almost as if he went to sleep while talking to me, though Collins got back quickly, he was dead.

TW recalls his final memory of his friend Tom Leary:

> *The last time I saw him, he was lying on his back in the snow. It was snowing very hard and his eyes and mouth were quickly covered. There was nothing anybody could do.*

Perhaps capturing the sentiments of the moment some fifty years later in a 1995 memorial service of the 94th Division Association, the Reverend Charles Manning (Company H , 301st Regiment) explained:

> Sorrow doesn't get more unbearable than when you see your best buddy that you were drafted with in 1942, a best buddy who had been in your presence at every experience since Camp Phillips, laying there beside you without an arm or a leg, or a head, with intestines all over the outside of his body, and in the height of your shock hear your squad leader's voice shouting "Keep moving, spread out, keep your head down, your eyes open, and your chin up." And so with tears running down your cheeks, your heart pounding with unbearable sorrow, a time when nothing was making sense, the Impossible Dream was getting a little closer to reality.

Following the loss of Goodlevege and Leary, Sergeant Collins found a sliver of fragment in a can of cheese in his backpack, and Lieutenant Reuter would later write his thoughts on the chance circumstances of life and death surrounding the incident:

> Actually, the shell could just as easily have killed all 10 of us. It was a huge shell and it landed right in our midst. It was a chance thing, depending on the break-up of the shell and where the pieces went…. I don't believe anyone was farther away from the explosion than Goodlevege, yet he caught one small fragment (a sliver) a fraction the size of the small jagged piece Collins took out of his can of cheese and it killed him instantly. A few inches over and it would have whipped past his ear leaving him completely unscathed.

Picture in TW's files, taken in Brittany, France. Decades ago, TW highlighted three faces in yellow, denoting killed in action: ❶ *Morris F. Faulkner from Georgia,* ❷ *Bernard Goodle-vege from Delaware, and* ❸ *Thomas R. Leary from Texas. TW highlighted one face in pink, denoting a wounded GI with the last name of* ❹ *Maferes.*

The 1ˢᵗ platoon spent that night in snow-filled foxholes, which Lieutenant Reuter later recalled as follows:

> By this time it was getting late and I put myself, Collins and Sam Harvey into a fox-hole of some size which was nearby and almost directly behind Sergeant Green and his last half-squad [including TW]. Green joined his group and we settled down to wait out the night. There was all sorts of strange sounds, noises and smells, and during the night it snowed, the flakes drifting down and making it difficult to watch. During one of my shifts awake and on guard, there was some noise and twigs breaking like a squad coming through the brush. I waited breathlessly and with increasing tension, thankful that Collins and Harvey didn't snore. It wasn't a German patrol—but that's another story. The following morning we knew that B Company had been captured.

While TW's Company E remained in the woods, Company B was forced to surrender, which the division history described as follows:

> Company B had almost exhausted its ammunition, the men were exhausted and freezing to death. Moreover, the area through which they would have to withdraw was heavily mined and their exact location was known to the enemy. For the sake of his remaining men, Captain Straub decided to surrender.

Other companies faced similar obstacles during the attack on Orscholz. The A Company's experience was recorded in the 94th Division history as follows:

> As the right of Company A slipped out of the woods and into the band of dragon's teeth, the stillness was broken by a series of loud explosions. Screaming in agony men fell among the concrete obstacles. Hidden beneath the thick carpet of snow was a field of Schu mines, S mines, and a tangle of barbed wire. Attempts to veer to the right and left only gave testimony to the extent and density of the minefield, though some few men were lucky enough to pass through the dragon's teeth unscathed.

The I Company did not fare much better:

> The assault units made progress until they encountered antipersonnel mines. As the artillery support lifted, the Germans laid their final protective line fires. Hidden machine guns raked the rifle platoons and casualties began to mount. The troops were finally withdrawn.

Noting that the pattern of "mines, booby traps, final-protective-line fire and accurate enemy artillery" repeated itself, the division history further describes the conditions facing TW and his fellow GIs:

> Throughout the night of the 20-21st, the German artillery relentlessly pounded the troops in the woods. Enemy shells crashed into the treetops and burst in deadly showers of shell fragments. By the time a count could be taken of the strength of a unit, additional casualties rendered the total incorrect. The group was gradually being whittled away. After darkness, those men caught in the draw during the day who had not frozen to death or been riddled by the almost constant machine gun and artillery fire, crawled back to the woods. Litter squads attempted to venture into the clearing time and again to remove the wounded, but repeatedly they were driven back by the volume of fire.

Many years ago, TW handwrote the name "Leary" next to the above paragraph in his copy of the 94th Division History.

Like TW's 2nd battalion, the 1st battalion of the 301st Regiment faced formidable opposition and was reduced from 1,000 men to less than 500, many of whom surrendered after being caught under heavy fire on open ground while further besieged by Schu mines buried under the deep snow. The Commander of the 1st battalion, Lieutenant Colonel Miller, was killed while trying to lead his men under impossible circumstances. As a result of overwhelming opposition, and perhaps lending credence to Hitler's declaration that "our strength lies in our intensive attacks and our barbarity," the Division History recorded the 94th Division's reluctant decision to cut its losses:

> Finally, Lieutenant Colonel Hardin called the regimental commander and in-

formed him it would take at least a regiment to accomplish the assigned mission. Permission was obtained to abandon the attack against Orscholz.

Never one to accept surrender, an incensed General Patton later asked the 94th Division regimental and battalion commanders "What happened to the battalion commander of the 400- 500 men and officers who had surrendered?" The response was given that "He was killed sir." With apparent satisfaction, Patton replied "Good, Good," after which he informed the officers that they were expected to lead their units, and to die with them as necessary.

Helen Keller once advised that "defeat is simply a signal to press onward." Despite the disaster at Orsholz, the 94th Infantry Division pressed on, with sentiments not unlike those of General George Washington, who during the darkest hours of the Revolutionary war, noted on December 24, 1776:

> I agree with you that it is vain to ruminate upon, or even reflect upon the authors of our present misfortunes. We should rather exert ourselves, and look forward with hopes, that some lucky chance may yet turn up in our favor.

General Patton similarly believed that "luck always changes if you do your best with what you have." Noting that "old scores were to be settled," the Division History indicates that one month later, the 94th Division returned and captured Orscholz. Soon after the events at Orscholz, TW was promoted to staff Sergeant, Platoon Guide. Fellow E-301, 1st Platoon veteran Lloyd Biser would later write in July 1977 that:

> Sergeant Smith was the platoon guide and assigned us to our positions. For about five days we were dug in and couldn't advance and the Germans likewise couldn't push us back. The weather was bitter cold and there was about eight or ten inches of snow on the ground.

As illustrated on the cover of this book, Sergeant TW soon found out that General Patton demanded that all officers, including non-commissioned officers like TW, wear their proper stripes, bars or stars on their helmets at all times. Believing that such a display turned officers into instant targets for German riflemen, Lieutenant Colonel George Whitman of the 376th Regiment, 94th Infantry Division, initially refused. Whitman later complied, noting "it took that third direct order before I did it." Whitman added however, that he was with Field Artillery Captain Davis just hours before "Captain Davis was found dead in a fox hole with a bullet hole between his two bars."

TW remembers a *class clown type* in his platoon whose helmet similarly provided a fatal target for German sharpshooters.

> *He always wore some sort of funny colored object on his helmet to amuse his fellow soldiers. One day while trekking through the snow, a number of shots were fired and his unforgettable helmet rolled past me.*

While lying in foxholes for extended periods of time, TW recalls his fellow GIs finding innovative ways to pass the time. TW remembers one GI in his unit who was a practical joker and emptied out the powder in a hand grenade.

> *In the middle of the night, the GI pretended like he heard something. He got up and tossed the grenade outside his foxhole. He started laughing when everyone else hit the dirt and covered themselves. To the GIs surprise, the grenade exploded. He had grabbed the wrong grenade. Fortunately, no one was hurt, but it scared the daylights out of him.*

TW also recalls waking up on many other occasions in the middle of the night when the Germans started up their tanks. The loud sound would wake up the GIs and cause them to be awake the rest of the night as they didn't know if an attack was coming. TW remembers other occasions where his platoon was advancing in the dark of night under low lying clouds, and the Germans would suddenly shine flood lights up from various directions to illuminate their American targets.

During this time, TW's training camp and ASTP buddy Gus Stavros was wounded and carried off the battlefield in Nennig, Germany, on January 19, 1945. Stavros noted that "we pushed the Germans out, then they would push us out; it was back and forth." Stavros was in the 3rd platoon, I Company, 376th Regiment, 94th Infantry Division. In February 1995, Stavros forwarded TW a letter he had just received from Russ Sanoden, who described the circumstances surrounding Stavros's injuries:

> A group of about 5 privates were called to help Sergeant (Kincaid?) take a group of German soldiers back from the front lines to an area where they could be handled and sent on to prison camps. I was one of those selected. It happened that I was just preparing a meal of C-rations when the call came. You came by my hole and said, "Oh Russ, you're just fixing your meal. I'll go for you." That was evidently accepted by the Sergeant. After some hours only one of the patrol returned, a tall, handsome Jewish soldier named Levensen, I think. His report was that the patrol had been struck by a shell, Sergeant Kincaid was killed and all of the others were wounded. He said that you had been hit by shrapnel in your head. There was no way we could locate where any of you men were. None ever returned to our unit. . . . . I want to thank you Gus from the bottom of my heart! You saved me from being badly wounded, and possibly from death by your kindness and your willingness to go in my place with those German prisoners.

Stavros was carried away in a stretcher, while saying prayers in Greek. He later underwent brain surgery and was flown to Paris, then London and then back to New York where he had a metal plate inserted in his head. He was partially paralyzed and notes that January 19, 1945, "was the last time I used my left hand." Despite predictions that he would have only a few years to live, he was fortunate to have received medical care from one of the Army's top brain surgeons, which would later enable him to live a long successful life. He received a Purple Heart and Bronze Star award and never returned to his unit.

Also fighting in Nennig, TW's Citadel friend and classmate, PFC Harry Bell Launius, Jr., was killed in action on January 27, 1945. The Division History notes that on the day Harry Launius was killed, German "machine guns and panzers that had stopped the American attack the preceding day went into action." Harry was a private infantry rifleman in the 302nd Regiment of the 94th Infantry Division. A memorial library dedicated by Harry's father in 1945 notes:

> Harry B Launius, Jr., honoree of the Memorial Library. Harry was a typical solider serving in WW II. He graduated with honors from Monroe High School in 1942. He spent a year at The Citadel before joining the Army in 1943. He was sent overseas in the summer of '44 and was killed in January of 1945. The news came to his family in four separate wires. The first reported that he was missing; the second said he was found alive, the third said he was missing, then the fourth confirmed his death at just 20 years of age.

Writing years later about Nennig, TW wrote:

> *Near a town called Nennig an unfortunate thing happened. There were a lot of dead German soldiers and the number of corpses increased. After the dead Americans were collected and removed, the dead Germans were collected and stacked neatly in a nearby house. Later the Germans counter-attacked and retook the area. Axis Sally reported on the German radio that these German prisoners of war were murdered in cold blood and branded the 94th Division as "Roosevelt's Bloody Butchers."*

94th Division troops in Nennig, which the History of the 94th Division notes "was littered with dead Krauts."

During the last week of January, intense fighting continued in Nennig, which like Berg and Wies, the U.S. took, lost, and then retook. Another of TW's ASTP buddies, Chuck Meyers, was a first scout in the E Company of the 376th Regiment at Nennig. Meyers survived Nennig, later writing to TW:

> After Nennig, I made squad leader. At the Saar Crossing at Ocken, I was promoted to platoon sergeant and took over the 3rd platoon of F/376 after they got wiped out.

Also during this time, in an effort to alleviate intense pressure in the Nennig area, General Malony prepared an order on January 25th authorizing an attack on the town of Sinz to the east. The Division History notes that the attack began at dawn the next morning "in a blizzard that added inches to the knee-deep snow." The third battalion of the 376th Regiment hit the first resistance, as noted in the Division History:

> There were more explosions and cries of agony. Schu mines! The platoon leader and several others had their feet blown off or badly mangled. Initial attempts at rescue succeeded only in setting off more mines.

The temperature remained bitter cold and additional men were being lost to trench foot and frostbite. Following continued artillery, attacks and casualties, Company G was reduced from 156 men to 45, and two other companies were reduced to "a combined strength of less than a single full-strength unit."

Instructions were later issued to withdraw the tanks from Sinz for other assignments. Without armored support, the Company Commander gave the order to pull back from Sinz while reinforcements were integrated, terrain was studied, and new plans devised.

During this time, the Division History notes that TW's "Second Battalion, 301st, commanded by Lieutenant Colonel Francis Dohs, remained on the Division's right flank, in the vicinity of Buschdorf and Hellendorf, temporarily attached to the 302nd." By January 30th, the 94th Division front line was held by TW's Second Battalion along with five other Battalions of the 301st and 302nd Regiments.

The Division History further notes that "when the 2nd Battalion, 301st Infantry, took over the positions in the Tettingen-Butzdorf area, Company E, commanded by Captain Walter J. Stokstad, went into defensive position in Untersie Busch and the woods southwest of Sinz supported by heavy machine guns of Lieutenant Walter J. Mulhall, Jr." Even with machine gun support, this was a dangerous area, and the Division History notes that "freezing temperatures and constant enemy shelling made life both miserable and hazardous." In addition to problems where "rifles actually froze and refused to function," causing at least one 94th infantryman "to urinate on my M-1 to free the action," the Division History further notes that "the area between Tettingen and Butzdorf was still hazardous during daylight hours as the enemy had unobstructed observation over this

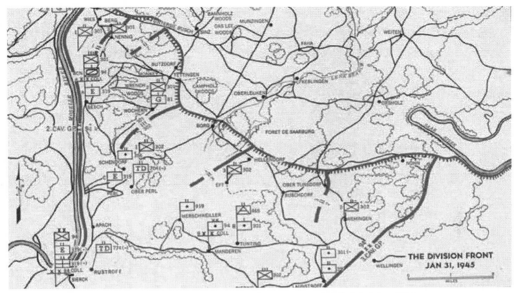

The Division Front, January 31, 1945. Source: 94th Division History

ground and his weapons were perfectly zeroed on it." TW's friend Bill Bird, K Company, 376th Regiment, 94th Infantry Division, found himself overrun by a German patrol near Sinz during a heavy snowfall in the middle of the night. On guard duty with his Browning Automatic Rifle (BAR), his rifle froze and would not fire, forcing his eventual surrender. Outnumbered and in total darkness, Bird recalls that his frozen BAR "may well have saved my life." He went on to endure two months of squalid, near starvation prison conditions, before being liberated by U.S. forces.

During this period, TW's friend Gus Allen was killed on February 2, 1945, in the Tettingen-Butzdorf area. Gus Allen was from Jamestown, New York, and entered the service while still a high school student, after which he was in the ASTP program and trained at Camp McCain with TW. In a 1989 letter to 301st Regiment veteran Doug Benson, TW recalled:

> *I sort of lost touch with Gus after we went into combat. As you know there was a lot of confusion. In February 1945 E company attacked Sinz, Germany. Before attacking Sinz, they sent out numerous patrols and I guess that's when Gus got it.*

Gus Allen was shot near the heart during a morning firefight while attacking a pillbox to divert attention so a demolition team could blow up the fortification. He was reportedly the only casualty during the patrol.

Meanwhile, General Patton was frustrated with his superior officers, Lieutenant General Omar Bradley and General Dwight Eisenhower, who disagreed with Patton's view that the division must aggressively press forward and attack despite fatigue and the infantry being under strength. Indeed, Patton's philosophy was more like that of General George Washington, who over 150 years earlier faced overwhelming odds and bleak conditions of rain, sleet and snow. Following the crossing of the Delaware River during which two of his men froze to death, one of Washington's commanding officers advised that the soldiers' guns were too soaked to fire, to which Washington responded, "Tell the general to use the bayonet."

TW recalls during this period one occasion where he was walking alone through a field when he happened upon the wreckage of an American plane. A few feet away, he noticed an American soldier lying on his back, the apparent victim of a German farmer armed with nothing but a pitchfork.

> *He must have survived the crash. He was probably injured, and the German just finished him off.*

TW also recalls a U.S. soldier from another regiment getting run over by a German Panzer. In another instance, TW and his GI buddies came across an abandoned German tank that had been destroyed.

> *The turret was busted open, and we were curious what was inside. I climbed up and thought I'd look for a weapon. There were dead German soldiers in there, and blood everywhere. Something had hit inside and looked like it had ricocheted.*

TW recalls that sights such as these were commonplace and that he and his fellow GIs just "*moved on.*" Quoting from British Prime Minister Winston Churchill:

> If you are going through hell, keep going.

A knocked out German Mark IV tank with part of it bazooka skirt still in place.
Source: 94th Division History

8. THE BATTLE OF SINZ

"My worst day of the whole war was on February 7, 1945. . . . That morning my platoon was almost full strength, over thirty men but by nightfall there were only six effectives left. However, we had taken and held the town of Sinz."

In early February, ten days of heavy rain turned foxholes into mud and ice. Meanwhile plans were being drafted for a 301st Regiment offensive to attack Sinz and the Bannholz Woods. This would be the second attack on Sinz, and the Division History notes that TW's 2nd Battalion "was given the lion's share of the regimental mission." Sinz was a small village with approximately one hundred and twenty houses, and the Division History notes that "the terrain over which the 2nd Battalion would attack was formidable... and definitely favored the defense." Remembering the February 6th march toward Sinz, Sergeant Jack Panes of Company G, 301st Regiment wrote:

> The trek through the woods was miserable: the complete blackness of the night; the slushing mud sticking to our shoepacs, making them heavier with every step; the nauseating stench of the dead who littered both sides of the road; and a fine, drizzling rain that accentuated the difficulty of our plight.

TW recalled in a 1999 letter that *"after going through the woods, we got replacements and on February 7, 1945 advanced into Sinz."*

Lieutenant Reuter would later recall that following more than a week of cold rainy weather, "we walked through mud up to our laces most of the way and went into position just east of the road in the woods—the first building in Sinz was just down the road—there were minefields etc. in between." The Division History recorded that:

> From the 2nd Battalion positions West to the river, the men of the 301st crouched in the mud and waited for the first light of dawn. When it came, Sinz and the woods around it erupted in a crash of American artillery; the infantry moved forward.

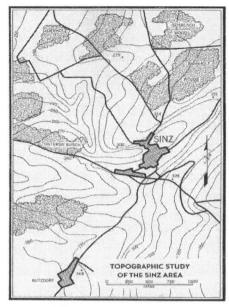
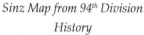

*Sinz Map from 94ᵗʰ Division
History*

*Note on photograph in TW's files: Medics
carry casualty of 301ˢᵗ Inf. 94ᵗʰ Div. Sinz*

Some of TW's most vivid WW II memories involved the bloody battle at Sinz. Years later, TW wrote of the experience:

> *My worst day of the whole war was on February 7, 1945. We were in fox holes on a hill overlooking a small German town, Sinz. . . . My platoon had just gotten replacements and with a few supporting troops there were almost forty of us. Not only our own artillery but also corps artillery shelled the town at 0700 and when it stopped we advanced into the town street fighting inch by inch.*

The Division History notes that as TW's Company E moved forward, "the troops were brought under intense mortar and artillery fire from the North. Far to the right, on the high ground overlooking the town four enemy tanks could be seen firing into Sinz. . . . The 1ˢᵗ and 2ⁿᵈ Platoons of Company E moved toward the buildings on their right flank, quickly eliminating some light opposition in the nearest houses, and taking twenty-two prisoners."

As the 1ˢᵗ and 2ⁿᵈ Platoons of Company E advanced on Sinz, the Division History notes that "at this point artillery, mortar and machine gun fire became intense." TW's friend and fellow E-301 rifleman Pfc. Fred W. Klein of Indianapolis, Indiana, was killed at Sinz on February 7, 1945. Fellow E-301 veteran Jim Mueller wrote of the incident in a May 1945 letter:

> Fred Klein was hit with a mortar shell. The company was going into an exposed draw which was under clear observation and as the string of platoons made their

Picture from TW's files of 94th Division soldiers taking cover at Sinz

way to cover they poured everything they had at them. At the same time and I believe the same round, Hinds was hit to.

Company E continued to advance through Sinz engaging in house-to-house fighting, soon taking an additional 15 prisoners. The Division History notes that "aided by heavy and constant artillery support, the company was slowly clearing its section of town. " During this time, TW's friend Hjalmar Lofblad of Grand View, Wisconsin, was killed. TW recalls that Hjalmar was married and had a young son. TW and Hjalmar Lofblad were taking cover inside a house when TW walked by an open window. As Hjalmar walked behind TW and past the same window, Hjalmar was shot in the back. TW recalls Hjalmar pointing and shouting obscenities at the Germans *"like I had never heard before in my life."* Those were his last words. Hjalmar Lofblad was awarded a silver star posthumously.

TW's platoon continued to advance through Sinz, as noted in the Division History:

Company E was the first to arrive at the road junction in the northern edge of Sinz which had been designated as the point of junction for the coordinated attacks launched by Companies E and G. Captain Stockstad's casualties had been such that he requested permission to delay at the initial objective until reinforcements could be brought forward. Battalion denied this request and the attack was pushed to the Northeast, to clear the remaining buildings in Sinz.

With orders to press on, the Division History further notes the progress of TW's platoon:

Company E moved out with the 1st Platoon on the left and the 2nd Platoon on the right of the street. The lead scout of the latter platoon was killed by rifle fire from one of the last buildings in town and at the same time four enemy machine guns opened fire from the outskirts of Sinz. This automatic fire was deadly and intense.

As the 1st platoon came under intense fire, TW was not far from Salvatore "Sam" D'Amico when D'Amico was shot in the eye. D'Amico was from Mahanoy City, Pennsylvania, and served in E-301 with TW.

Sam said he'd been shot, and he was holding his hand over his eye. I told him there were many guys much worse off and that there was a lot that doctors could do for the eye. Sam pulled his hand away and was holding his eye in his hand. He said "they're not going to fix this one." I didn't know what the heck to do. I helped escort him out of there.

TW's friend Joseph Platko of Monessen, Pennsylvania, was killed soon after, and TW adds *"Every time I turned around, something else was happening. It was overwhelming."* Guy Fisher of Company G likewise recalled of the fighting at Sinz: "Existing in extreme cold, under fire and surrounded by dead men, some horribly mutilated, had a debilitating effect on us."

At one point during the fighting at Sinz, TW recalls exchanging pistol fire with a German soldier who was at the other end of a long alley lined with houses.

The German soldier was shooting at me with a Luger pistol. I returned fire with my Colt 45 caliber revolver. My gun had more firepower than the German Luger and the echo was so loud in that alley that it sounded like a canon. The German turned around and ran. I don't think I ever saw him again.

Later during the fighting at Sinz, TW also remembers running into a large stone house with an arch in an effort to find cover and avoid gunfire.

At one point mortar shells started dropping everywhere. There was no roof on the house where I was. I noticed that although the house was destroyed across the street there was a deep stone opening to the cellar of the house. While the shells were bursting about me I ran across the street down a few steps into the cellar. Bumped into something. I had been holding my rifle diagonally in front of me. What I bumped into was a German soldier and the muzzle of my rifle was under his chin. He dropped his rifle and yelled "Kammerad." Stayed in the cellar with the German for several hours during the shelling. He admitted he had been shooting at me. Said the "feld wevel" (field sergeant) assigned him there. I asked him where the sergeant was and he said "gefallen" which means he's gone. Don't remember where he was from but he said that before the war he was a carpenter.

TW recalls that there was a dead German soldier on the couch in the basement. After the shelling stopped, he and the German prisoner ventured out of the basement:

After the shooting stopped, I was marching the captured German soldier out of the town. At one point, the German stopped abruptly. I told him to keep moving. He refused. He then pointed to a land mine in the field in front of them. I think we would both be dead if we had continued.

The experience with the German prisoner was TW's only favorable recollection of an encounter with a German soldier, and it may well have saved TW's life. TW also noted that he had walked through part of that same field earlier that day. TW eventually took the soldier around the field and turned him in with another group of prisoners. TW recalls the German soldier shaking his hand when TW turned him over and the soldier said "auf wiedersehen." Also during this time, TW "liberated" a German Luger pistol from another German prisoner. After the war, TW traded the Luger for a new German Walther PPK, which is the type of pistol Hitler used to kill himself.

Another experience of taking a German prisoner at Sinz was relayed by TW's friend Peter SanFillipo. SanFillipo served with TW in Company E, 301st Regiment, and he was one of the three GIs who posed earlier for a picture with TW in front of Big Ben and the House of Parliament in 1944. In a 1989 94th Division Commemorative History, SanFillipo recalled:

While occupying Sinz, a patrol was ordered to enter the nearby woods and make contact with the enemy. The patrol moved out, and I was in the rear as follow up. As I skirted along the road, I noticed a dead German soldier in the roadside ditch. I could not be sure whether our patrol had killed him, or whether he had been there for some time. I did notice he had side-arms consisting of a P-38 and a trench knife. I decided to check him out and as I attempted to remove his pistol, he suddenly came alive and exclaimed "they're mine, the weapons are mine!" I told him, "The hell they are, they are mine!" We struggled and I put my rifle to his stomach and still stuttering from the shock of his coming to life, I told him he was my prisoner.

TW recalls one point after midnight during the fighting at Sinz when Lieutenant Reuter was hit by a mortar shell and TW and others dragged him to shelter. Recalling the incident years later, Lieutenant Reuter wrote:

The 1st platoon was on the left or East side going house to house along this dirt secondary street next to Bannholz Woods. It was the last house that decimated the 1st platoon, however, I was gone by then…. I had been dragged into the protection of a German bunker and Sergeants Green and Collins had posted Tom

Picture from TW's files of 94th Division GIs at Sinz, Germany

Smith to stand guard over me, until I could be evacuated…. I do think my being blown away when I was may have been one of the best things that's happened to me—and also for Tom Smith. Considering what happened later, the odds are good that it may have saved both our lives.

TW recalls that after Lieutenant Reuter was wounded, Sergeant James W. Green from Kentucky led the 1st platoon. Writing years later in a December 1, 1998, letter to Lieutenant Reuter, TW would note of Sergeant Green:

He was the most impressive combat soldier I have ever met. I have seen him pick up and throw back German hand grenades that had been thrown at us over a hedge row. I have seen him while shooting kick down doors, climb thru windows, fire a bazooka and use a flame thrower in street fighting.

Sergeant Green (right) shared TW's good fortune in surviving Sinz, and one of his experiences with TW and the 1st Platoon is described in the Division History as follows:

The platoon planned to throw all available fire power against the building, then rush the position. Noiselessly, the men inserted full clips into their weapons and waited the word to open fire. Suddenly, the Germans, who had hatched a similar plan, let go with everything they had.

The Americans immediately replied in kind. Sergeant Green was moving from the house by way of a window when there was a terrific blast in the room behind him; he was blown to the ground. An enemy Panzerfaust had penetrated the wall of the building and exploded. . . . Of the three men in the room Sergeant Green had been leaving, all had been killed; six others in the house had been knocked unconscious by the explosion of the Panzerfaust.

The 1st Platoon was engaged in heavy combat the entire day and into the night, as noted in the Division History:

By midnight Sinz quieted as the artillery, mortar and rocket fire slackened. For the following two and a half hours, enemy fire continued only intermittently, but at 0230 hours the tempo increased. From then until 0400 hours Sinz was pounded with everything the German artillery could bring to bear. What few roofs remained intact were soon riddled. Fires broke out and the sky above Sinz reddened.

The 301st Regiment pressed on, and the 94th Infantry Division Combat Narrative reports that "the 301st Infantry fought house-to-house and captured Sinz February 7-8, 1945." In an August 17, 1995, letter to a veteran major of the 94th division, TW recalled:

That morning my platoon was almost full strength, over thirty men, but by nightfall there were only six effectives left. However we had taken and held the town of Sinz.

Fellow E-301, 1st platoon veteran Lloyd Biser likewise wrote years later that:

Finally at the urging of General Patton and with the assistance of Corps artillery we advanced taking most of Sinz. However in one day's time our platoon was reduced from about forty two men and an officer to but six men and we were relieved.

Consistent with TW and Biser's recollection, TW's platoon was decimated by the end of the battle, as later published in the Division History's account of the Sinz attack:

Staff Sergeant Green, who was now leading the 1st Platoon [of E-301], counted his men. The task was quickly completed as the platoon numbered exactly six effectives. All of the men had armed themselves with BARs [Browning Automatic Rifles].

The other 36 men of the E-301 first platoon were killed, wounded or captured, but the town of Sinz was "now completely in American hands." Company G also took heavy casualties, as later remembered by Sergeant Jack Panes of Company G, 301st Regiment:

Sinz was just a small town with about 120 houses. Yet, for every one taken at least one man in G Company had to pay one way or another.

According to a March 1945 Army Ground forces report, "on 7 February after the woods had been gained the 94th took Sinz in a bloody action." An Army Times Combat

Division summary report likewise singles out Sinz as "bloody fighting," and the battle's toll on the 301st Regiment is noted in the Division History:

> By noon on the 8th of February, all units engaged in the Sinz area were operating at greatly reduced strength. In addition to the losses in dead and wounded, the constant artillery and mortar fire on the town, which was averaging two to three rounds a minute, produced numerous cases of combat exhaustion.

Remembering what was left of the town, Sergeant Jack Panes explained that "Sinz wasn't much of a town to start with; it was no town when we finished." TW's friend Bob Bowden, who was from Connecticut and served in a patrol unit associated with the E-301 second platoon before being assigned as a replacement near the end of the battle of Sinz, remembers that Sinz was "most dramatic, very physically and emotionally difficult, just an experience that stays in the minds of most of us."

Later recalling the events of Sinz, Lieutenant Reuter would write:

> Sinz was the nastiest place I encountered during World War II. There was everything there—tank traps, dragon's teeth, shoe mines, teller mines, bunkers, SS panzer units, tiger tanks, etc.

TW likewise recalls that Sinz was *the most awful place I have ever been.* He later adds, *"actually, I never thought I'd survive."*

Picture from TW's files of Sinz, Germany during WW II

9. REPLACEMENTS

"Sometimes a replacement was killed before I even knew his name."

After the fighting in Sinz, Lieutenant Dohs assembled men to attack Bannholz Woods. The men again encountered overwhelming opposition, and the Division History noted that one platoon of company G sent its final radio transmission saying "the tanks are moving down the line, with infantry, firing into each foxhole." Reflecting the physical and mental state of the 301st Regiment, which among other tactics had "continued to advance by employing marching fire," the Division History notes:

> Survivors of the four groups that had gone into the woods were physically and mentally strained from hours of close fighting, constant artillery pounding and front-line existence. They were exhausted, thoroughly and completely. Many of the men were on the verge of cracking and some could not even remember their own names.

By February 9th, the Division History noted that "the Commanding Officer of the 2nd Battalion, his staff and men were bordering on exhaustion. Their supporting artillery was also beginning to tire; in seventy-two hours of fighting, the 356th Field Artillery alone had expended 6,965 rounds of 105 mm ammunition." Multiple attacks from different regiments failed, and Lieutenant Colonel Whitman of the 376th Regiment remembered that "of the 127 men and officers of my company that participated in the attack on Bannholz Woods on February 10, 1945, only twenty-seven or so came out with me." Between the 9th and 14th of February, the Division History notes that:

> The enemy continued to deluge Campholz with perfectly adjusted artillery and mortar fire; mines and booby traps which were thickly strewn throughout the area inflicted occasional casualties. The weather remained cold and wet. Mud in the woods was knee-deep in places and holding the position was a dirty, dangerous task.

Describing the condition of Companies F and G, the Division History notes:

It was a pitifully small group to be called two companies. Many of the men had lost their weapons and equipment. They were all mud-covered, stunned, hollow-eyed and exhausted after hours in a hell of flying steel, impotent against the repeated close-in attacks of the German armor.

Despite these conditions, the Division pressed forward and Staff Sergeant Voit observed that "The marching fire demonstration put on by our doughs was a thing of weird beauty. The men seemed to forget about mines or opposing fire. . ." The Division History further notes that:

> To summarize, during the period from January 7, 1945, when the Division took over positions in the Triangle, to February 15, 1945, the men of the 94th had practically destroyed the 416th Infantry Division, reduced the infantry and tank strength of the 11th Panzer Division by one-half, prevented the disengagement of sizable portions of enemy armor for the employment elsewhere, and compelled the diversion of badly needed German infantry replacements to the Siegfried Switch.

On February 12, 1945, TW's Citadel friend, Second Lieutenant Martin Frederick ("Jack") Schnibben, Jr., was killed while being held as a German prisoner. Following his graduation from The Citadel in May 1943, Lt. Schnibben was married in July 1943 and then served in the Eighth Regiment of the Army's Fourth Infantry Division in WW II. On February 11, 1945, Lieutenant Schnibben's wife was notified that her husband was missing in action. Three months later, she received a letter from Lt. Schnibben's buddy notifying her that Jack was wounded in both legs and then captured after his unit was forced to retreat following a German advance. Finally, on August 6, 1945, Mrs. Schnibben was notified that her husband was killed in action on February 12th while a German prisoner. Like TW, Lt. Schnibben had served in England, France and Germany and had entered combat in 1944.

On February 21, 1945, General Malony wrote to his 94th Division men:

> Your successes have had a great effect upon the War. You have practically annihilated two German divisions and have reduced the combat efficiency of a third (Panzer Division) to a small fraction of its original efficiency. You have captured 2,851 prisoners and wrested from the enemy more than 65 miles of wealthy, productive country.

TW's 301st Regiment was involved in a number of bloody battles during this period, which were described in a 1944-45 *Stars and Stripes* publication on the 94th Division as follows:

> Headed for the Saar, the 301st and 302nd swept aside all opposition. Hilly terrain offered Germans a good spot for artillery and anti-tank guns in covering roads and likely routes of approach, but doughfeet were determined to reach the Saar

TW somewhere in France or Germany

and artillery guns weren't going to stop them. One squad of the 301st knocked out six 88s and their crews in a stretch of 200 yards.

While TW was in Germany, he recalls entering one German town and coming across an 88 German cannon that had been firing at the US soldiers and was tilted over.

> *I saw a German citizen and called him over and asked where the soldiers were who were firing the cannon. I knew enough German to ask the question in German. The man replied in perfect English "I don't know, but if I knew I would not tell you." I got a kick out of that.*

In addition to combat injury and death, many GIs suffered non-combat fatalities due in large part to the dangerous equipment and weapons that GIs were handling. TW's friend Ellwood Thompson of Capitol Heights, Maryland, and also a member of the 301st Infantry Regiment, survived the Battle of Sinz but was killed shortly thereafter. The two men were from the D.C. area and shared the name Thompson, which was TW's mother's maiden name. In fact, they often speculated that they might be related. On February 22, 1945, TW and some of his fellow soldiers were vying for a free weekend pass to Paris.

Three days prior to Ellwood Thompson's death, U.S. Marines landed on Iwo Jima in the Pacific. The United States completed the capture of the island in March 1945, following nearly a month of fighting and the loss of 20,000 American soldiers.

Elwood Thompson was the winner of the coveted prize, which would provide a brief respite from the war and the frequent fear of injury and death.

> *Shortly after winning the pass, Elwood took off his jacket in excitement, at the same time accidentally triggering a hand grenade and blowing himself up. I don't remember why, but I had left the room prior to that point.*

Recalling the circumstances of Thompson's death, fellow E-301 veteran Jim Mueller wrote about the event a few months later in a May 1945 letter:

> In that room where we were when that grenade went off a number of the boys were hit too. Thompson was killed outright since the thing went off close to his head. Fay Freeman was hurt in his head there too and we were told that he lost the sight of both eyes. That is really too bad because he was a guy that would have a hard time to get along without them. Also that grenade put a few holes into Flack's stomach and they say he is making out okay. Those are the serious ones in that deal and Lollis, Rochford, and a couple replacements got a few scratches. I was there but somehow came out with just a headache.

Remembering the incident 64 years later, TW concludes:

> *I guess when it is your time to go, it is your time to go. That's about all I could conclude from that.*

With reference to non-combat injuries, the Reverend Manning noted in a 2008 memorial service for the 94th Infantry Division Association:

> General Patton once told General Malony that the 94th Infantry Division had more "non-combat" casualties than any unit that he had commanded in his entire career in the Army. Patton then went on to tell General Malony that if he didn't do something about it that he would become a "non-combat casualty" himself.

Many have observed that it would have been futile, if not suicidal, to point out to General Patton that the failure of his staff to provide appropriate winter clothes and shoes was a root cause of the large majority of "non-combat casualties." As the war pressed on, WW II noncombat injuries in the U.S. armed forces remained constant at about fifty to one hundred injuries per thousand GIs. Combat injuries, however, steadily increased. WW II combat injuries started at one per thousand in early 1942 and increased to between fifty and one hundred injuries per thousand while TW was in Europe in late 1944 and 1945. By war's end, over 650,000 GIs had been wounded.

During the last six months of 1944, between twelve and eighteen thousand GIs were killed each month, exceeding the Army's casualty estimates. In early 1945, the 94th Division remained engaged in heavy combat and suffered significant combat casualties, requiring more replacement troops than expected or available. TW's friend Bob Bowden remembers that:

> It was a difficult time. I saw people get shot. I saw people dead. I saw people in all stages of human conduct, some extremely heroic, some who were less than that. It took a lot of guts. We took shelter down in cellars; it was rough with shells pounding on walls. You'd keep down as low as you could and hope you didn't get hit.

Referring to Patton's unrelenting drive and use of replacements, Leon Standifer of Company K, 301st Regiment, explained in a 94th Division Commemorative History that:

> Even today, I feel uncomfortable defending Patton. He looked on riflemen as comparable to spare parts for his tanks: when they wore out he simply replaced them.

In a February 15, 1945, phone call between XX Corps Major General Walton H. Walker and 94th Division Major General Harry J. Malony, the concern of Major General Malony was apparent as he noted with some trepidation his need for more replacements, including "riflemen."

> *Malony:* Have you got time for me to tell you a little information? I will have to use Hagerty again. He has just been three days. His is the 301st. Actually I have been splitting replacements between him and McClune; they are about equally down. I am shy about 600 men; particularly, I am shy platoon leaders, about 90 of them. My proportion of new men is about 70%. I want you to know our status.
> *Walker:* I do and I do know that your outfit is shot pretty badly.
> *Malony:* Well, I just wanted you to know.
> *Walker:* I do know Harry, I watch it and check on it all the time. . . .
> *Malony:* I am trying to do this thing for you just as hard as God will let me. I just wanted you to know the situation.
> *Walker:* From now on there is no question about defense. From now on we will go forward; there will only be attacks.

Malony: I have had casualties, about 4,000 now, and my battle casualties are about 2,200. As to the time, I have some reinforcements that are due tomorrow morning, about 175 of them, and I will have to use them.

Walker: Not immediately, are you?

Malony: I will have to.

Walker: Why?

Malony: Because I'm so damned short in riflemen.

This was a critical problem, because as pointed out by 301st Regiment veteran Leon Pate Johnson, writing years later for the 94th Infantry Division in an historical review, "In summary, gentlemen, wars are won by the soldier on the ground—the infantry man— the backbone of the small unit." Expressing similar sentiments in the 94th Division Commemorative History, 301st Regiment veteran William Warren explained:

> The progress of a war is measured by the location of its front-line troops. That's the Infantry! Every weapon a country possesses, its ships, its airplanes, the artillery, and yes, the tanks, are all there for one purpose, to assist the Infantry to close with the enemy.

While some 16 million men and women served in WW II, there were only eighty-nine Divisions that participated in WW II ground warfare. Thirty-eight percent of enlisted personnel had "rear echelon" jobs, such as administrative or technical support, and only one in ten soldiers saw combat. As Tom Brokaw points out, "the ratio of men in infantry divisions to those in backup positions was one to four," and "only a small fraction [of those in uniform during WW II] were directly exposed to enemy fire." General Patton knew full well the importance of the front line troops and was quick to deflect credit for the Third Army's success during the Battle of the Bulge:

> We hit the sons of bitches on the flank and stopped them cold. Now that may sound like George Patton is a great genius. Actually he had damned little to do with it. All he did was to give orders.

General Omar Bradley explained the plight of the infantry rifleman who carried out these orders on the front lines:

> The rifleman fights without promise of either reward or relief. Behind every river there's another hill—and behind that hill, another river. After weeks or months in the line only a wound can offer him the comfort of safety, shelter, and a bed. Those who are left to fight, fight on, evading death but knowing that with each day of evasion they have exhausted one more chance for survival. Sooner or later, unless victory comes, this chase must end on the litter or in the grave.

With often insufficient resources, the 94th Division pressed on with replacements and perseverance. Writing of his experience with front line replacements in a 94th Infantry Division Commemorative History, Bill Jones of Company F, 301st Regiment noted:

> During a short period of 2 days and nights, I signed for the replacements and arbitrarily assigned them to the platoons and squads with the largest holes in their lines. Platoon runners took the men to any available squad leaders. I saw replacements old enough to be my father. Some of them were so small they could not physically handle an M1. All ranks were included: Privates, Sergeants and 2nd Lieutenants. And essentially all of them had been "drafted" from rear echelon, non-combat army units.

TW recalls that one of his assignments as a Sergeant during the war was to escort replacements out to the line of fire. TW remembers that some of them had never seen combat before and were crying as he escorted them past fellow dead GIs, and TW adds *"that didn't help any."* TW also recalls that *"some of the replacements died that same day, including some that never made it out to the front line."*

Relaying his own experience as a replacement, 94th Infantry Division replacement Don Multry, who served in the F Company of the 301st Regiment, wrote to TW on March 29, 1990, noting:

> I joined the 94th Infantry Division somewhere between Sinz and the Saar. My ignorance is perhaps bliss, but replacements were in total ignorance. If they lasted, they would learn who is who and what is what in the course of time. I was hospitalized due to a combination of a million dollar wound and a developing attack of appendicitis.

In an effort to put a more positive spin on the replacement situation, Dave Bell remembered that

> After some months, they started calling them 'reinforcements' instead of 'replacements.' They were always trying to influence our minds.

Noting the difference between replacements and an experienced infantryman, E-301 Lieutenant Reuter wrote:

> With mortar rounds you had no warning at all until it was above your head—a split 1/100th of a second before it hit. With artillery, you at least heard it coming and an infantryman soon learned to judge where the shell was going to land within a few yards shortly after he heard its approach…. The new marveled at the coolness of the old hands during artillery barrages—when it was really experience—they knew where the shells would land. It was an instinct the new

Picture from TW's files of 94th Division GIs during the Battle of the Bulge

arrivals soon acquired if they lived through their first few barrages. Unfortunately, the talent had little civilian application, except to help insure you had the opportunity to be one again.

In one particular incident, TW remembers escorting a replacement out and giving him a bazooka *"because he was big and I thought he could handle it."* He shot it at a tank and *"only attracted attention."* The German soldiers, walking alongside their tanks, spotted him and shot and killed him. *"I had just met him that day."*

In another instance during the war, TW recalls serving as the Platoon Guide in charge of directing the troops where to go. TW remembers being crouched behind a wall with fellow GIs *"somewhere in Europe, during the conflict."*

> *We were all down. One of the replacements who was at the end of the wall called me over to him saying "Look...Look!" So I crawled over to him to see what he had spotted. The next thing I knew he was shot in the face and killed as he was talking right next to me and peering around the wall... Sometimes a replacement was killed before I even knew his name. I decided we'd go a different direction.*

In addition to escorting replacements to the front line, TW and other 94th Division GIs often escorted German prisoners from the front line. Managing prisoners could prove difficult, and Lieutenant Reuter relayed one of his own experiences attempting to take prisoners:

> They put both hands on their helmets. I could barely see them and I had no opportunity to take their sidearms, which as machine gunners, they would have had. These were still 11th Panzer Division people, not Volksturm, and they quickly feigned total stupidity and lack of any knowledge of "Halt!" in any language, including German. I realized they had really taken charge of me and were leading me down the hill, rather than vice-versa. Soon they would be in the brush where I couldn't see them, and they refused to halt, pretending ignorance

of what I wanted. At the last instance, I shot them both, the lead one first just before he would have been out of my sight. I quickly moved out of line, so there was little possibility of being hit should there be return fire.

As German casualties continued to mount, 94th division casualties remained high during this period, but phone records of a February 21, 1945, conversation between the two Major Generals continued to reflect an unrelenting determination and drive by the Army and its commanders:

Malony: We will need a helluva lot of luck.

Walker: We have had luck. We always had luck. That is Johnny Walker luck. That is known throughout the Army. I wouldn't be a Corps Commander if I didn't have it. I think it is going thru. Whether or not it does, it is a masterpiece so far and just go on and SPEED AND POWER. Goddamn, push them. As long as you got one man left. . . . .

General Patton recognized that "we have to push people beyond endurance in order to bring the war to an end." Exclaiming that "I shall drive you until hell won't have it," Patton demanded that his men "go forward until the last round is fired and the last drop of gas is expended. . . .then go forward on foot."

The United States successfully regained all lost ground during the Battle of the Bulge, which officially ended on January 28, 1944 and was the largest battle fought by the Americans in World War II. Describing the event, Patton noted that "during this operation, the Third Army moved farther and faster and engaged more divisions in less time than any other army in the history of the United States—possibly in the history of the world." The battle was particularly brutal, with American casualties of 81,000 men and German casualties of 100,000 men. British Prime Minister Winston Churchill described the battle as "the greatest American battle of the war [which] will, I believe, be regarded as an ever famous American victory."

10. TRENCH FOOT, FROSTBITE AND HOSPITALS

"Trench foot and frostbite saved my life."

TW recalls a bitter cold winter with frequent ice, rain and snow, causing even General Patton to wonder "how human beings could endure this continuous fighting at sub-zero temperatures is still beyond my comprehension." These conditions presented many obstacles for GIs, and it has been suggested that terrain and weather were nearly as formidable as the Nazis. Although manufacturing companies had been identified to convert mattress covers to snow suits, TW remembers using whatever they could find as camouflage in the snow, including *"white sheets and tablecloths."*

GIs were spending extended periods of time in snow, wet conditions and foxholes lined with "icy mud." As a result of cold weather, wet conditions, and insufficient shoes, by the end of April 1945, over 44,000 U.S. soldiers experienced trench foot and frozen feet. The Division History noted that:

> Frost bite and trench foot which, in spite of every precaution, dogged the 94th from its initial day on the Western Front, continued to take their toll of casualties…. Moreover, the constantly alternating pattern of snow and bitter cold, rain and mud sapped the vitality of the troops.

HQ/301 Men Wear Bed Sheets for Camouflage in the Nennig-Sinz area.

In addition to the extreme cold, inadequate shoes contributed to the problem, and the Division history notes that "ever since the Division had reached the Western Front, lack of proper foot gear for work in the snow, during the dead of a very cold winter, had caused an excessive number of non-battle casualties." The problem was so bad that GIs learned to take the warmer and dryer boots from German soldiers. Some GIs disputed that these were "non-combat" casualties. Writing of the frozen feet problem in a 94th Division Historical Review, Leon Standifer of the K Company of the 301st Regiment noted:

> Those of us who lay in frozen ditches and foxholes knew that our feet were frozen, and that it was a direct result of enemy action. If they hadn't been shooting at us we could have moved around, or even built a fire. . . . The official history of the Quartermaster Corps in the ETO calls the combat boot problem a most serious miscalculation. The total combat boot problem cast an equivalent of all the riflemen of seven infantry divisions. Thousands of young men had their feet amputated, thousands have spent every winter since in pain.

Robert Adair of the I Company of the 376th Regiment similarly noted:

> With the constant shellfire, we were forced to stay in the trenches where the low spots were always filled with water, iced over sometimes during the day and always at night.

Writing of the 302nd Regiments' experience with trench foot in early February 1945, the 94th Division History noted that "many of the men were so crippled with trench foot that walking was sheer agony." Remembering the freezing conditions, 94th Division veteran Bob Higgins speculated in a 94th Division Association article "how many of our comrades suffered and died not because of the minor wounds they received but because they were subject to the snow and the freezing temperatures? They fell in the snow and died from exposure." On a lighter note, Higgins recalled the Army-issued cold weather gear, noting:

> Dressed like that, relieving one's self was a time consuming and chilling operation. First of all, one had a talk with one's self as to whether this trip was really necessary or could it be held off for another hour or so.

The relevance of this observation is apparent when reading one of the recollections of a January 1945 night in Germany later written by Lieutenant Reuter of TW's E-301 1st platoon:

> Some of the more memorable things I recall, other than the peaceful, snow-covered setting. . ., it seemed after dark the 1st Platoon had a rather serious bout with diarrhea for a few days.

Perhaps selectively, this particular memory was lost on TW.

Note on photograph in TW's files: "Infantry men of the 94th Division advance on Sinz. Here they are taking cover in a muddy ditch beside the road to escape an enemy barrage. 301st Inf., Feb. 7, 1945"

The cold and wet weather eventually took its toll on many GIs in the Battle of the Bulge, including TW.

> *I spent most of the winter outside, and much of it in foxholes with mud and melted snow at the bottom. I understand there also was a problem with our shoes. They absorbed water. Eventually I got trench foot and frostbite.*

Years later, TW wrote of his experience with trench foot and frostbite.

> *As I was escorting the wounded and prisoners back to the Battalion, Chaplan grabbed me by the arm and said "You are going to the medics." I didn't realize it but at the time I was limping. The medics removed my shoes. My feet were swollen, black and yellow and cracking on the bottom. It was trench foot, frozen feet and frostbite. The medics carried me piggyback to an evacuation area. There along with several other GIs, we were placed in an ambulance. We were driven to a hospital in Thoinville, France. I was placed flat on my back in a bed but my feet were left elevated and uncovered. We were instructed not to get out of bed, not even stand. Several times a day doctors would come by, examine our feet and scratch on them. The ward was called the "bull pen" for almost every day someone's toe, foot or leg was amputated and in most cases they were sent to England or the United States. My feet thawed out although it was painful.*

TW was admitted to the 92nd medical evacuation hospital on February 15, 1945. Despite being warned of the possible need for amputation, TW was fortunate that his feet improved quickly and he was able to return to his unit. Tragically, the soldier who was brought in to replace TW in the regiment was killed in action one week later. As a consequence, TW speculates that:

> *Trench foot and frostbite saved my life.*

Another 301st Regiment soldier, Dick Simmers, who commanded Company K, was likewise sent to the hospital with trench foot and frostbite, in addition to a serious head wound. The doctors urged Simmers to amputate both feet or risk likely death from gangrene. Simmers refused and was fortunate to have survived, although with extreme pain in his feet every winter.

Despite having trench foot and frostbite and living and sleeping outside in bitter, icy cold for weeks on end, TW notes in amazement:

> *I never got sick, not even a cold.*

Referencing trench foot and frost bite in a March 1945 phone call between Major General Walton Walker, XX Corps, and Major General Harry Malony, 94th Division, Harry Malony reported on the 94th Division's progress, noting that things are "going swell right now." In reply, Major General Walker noted:

> Goddamn, I sure like to hear those words. You can wear your flag from now on. Trench foot and frost bite—goddamn, you have gone like a house on fire. . . .Harry, you are doing wonderful work. I will kiss you when I see you…. Keep going, fellow, goddamn it.

In addition to trench foot and frostbite, the Division History notes that by March, one regiment found that "mines, mortars and artillery fire accounted for the greatest share of the total casualties" and that "many of the casualties were from Schu mines which characteristically blew off one or both feet or mangled them to the point where amputation was necessary." TW's friend Bob Bowden of the second platoon of E-301 later volunteered for a patrol unit and recalled casualties from tree bursts of mortar and shell fire, as well as schu mines that he remembers blew the foot off one man in his patrol. Recalling the casualties and risks, Bowden notes:

> They knew the territory a lot better than we did; we walked into it for the first time, but they knew every valley, nook and trail. We had large scale maps, but we didn't know where we were half the time.

While TW was in the hospital with trench foot, Lieutenant Colonel Hardin, the 301st Regiment Executive Officer, was wounded by shell fragments on February 21st and was evacuated. A couple days later, Lieutenant Colonel Dohs, who commanded the 2nd Battalion and reported to Lieutenant Colonel Hardin, was "killed instantly by almost a direct hit from one of the enemy shells" at the Staadt Crossing on February 23rd. On the same day, Captain Stockstad, who commanded Company E and reported to Lieutenant Colonel Dohs, was left in the care of medics after he and others in the battalion collapsed from exhaustion. Also on that day, Captain Sinclair of Company F, 301st Regiment, was mortally wounded, noting before he died "it took a big one to get me." Lieutenant Colonel Dohs was awarded the Distinguished Service Cross posthumously.

Battle and non-battle injures remained a daily fact of life and TW recalled an earlier incident before the Battle of the Bulge when he went to visit his childhood friend and fellow Camp Hood and ASTP buddy Graham Northrup, whom he had referenced in his first letter home from Europe. Graham Northrup was in Company F of the 302nd Regiment and had been wounded and hospitalized in France. He was injured by friendly fire when a mortar misfired and fell short of its target, severely injuring Northrup's hand. Northrup later wrote that "I was wounded in 24 places by a mortar burst," and noted that the officer responsible for the incident personally apologized to him as Northrup was being carried away to a hospital. TW's chance encounter with another Smith during that same visit was reflected in a Fall 1989 issue of the 94th Infantry Division Association's newsletter, *The Attack*, as follows;

> T.W. Smith, E/301, lives in Falls church, Va., and T.W. Smith, F/301, is from Gadsden, Ala. The two met by chance 45 years ago in November 1944 in a U.S. Army hospital in Rennes, France. The Virginia T.W. went to the hospital to visit a wounded buddy [Graham T. Northrup] and in checking the hospital records trying to locate his friend's room, he was startled at seeing his name "T.W. Smith" listed as a patient. Knowing how the Army sometimes operates, he wondered if it might possibly be an "advance reservation," so down the corridor he marched to "his" room to check it out. That is how the chance meeting occurred. Sitting up in bed was T.W. Smith from Alabama, who was not only pleased at having a visitor but really taken by surprise upon learning his visitor was also named T.W. Smith.

TW never had another opportunity to meet the other TW Smith, whom TW recalls was badly wounded at the time.

The article in *The Attack* went on to note that the 94th Infantry Division Association lists the names of 10,000 94th infantry veterans, including 57 Smiths, two of which have the first initial "TW" as noted above. This may explain the Western Union telegram TW's parents received on February 3, 1945 stating that their son Sergeant Thomas Warner Smith was slightly injured in action in Germany. TW's picture was included in the Washington Times-Herald on February 17, 1945, under the headline "Nine Killed, 19 Hurt, Two Missing Among Soldiers from D.C. and Near-by Areas." TW was not injured on February 3, 1945, and believes the telegram to his parents related to another Smith and was mistakenly sent to his parents.

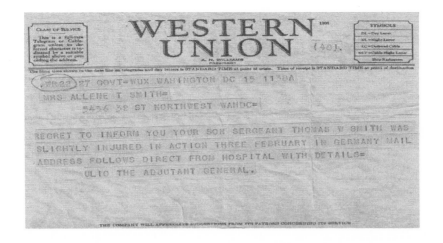

TIMES-HERALD

Nine Killed, 19 Hurt, Two Missing Among Soldiers From D. C. and Near-by Areas

Manassas Family Loses Second Son

Continued from Page 17

Wingo, First Lieut. Hugh C. Bowers.

WOUNDED

Pfc. Nathan A. Emmons, 24, Thirty-sixth Infantry, husband of Mrs. Gertrude Emmons, 1024 Sixteenth St. North, Arlington, son of Mr. and Mrs. Charles B. Emmons, Groveton, Va. (Wounded January 24, France.)

Pfc. Raymond Weiss, 28, son of Rose and Herman Weiss, 813 Sixth St. NW. (Wounded January 5, Luxemburg.)

Lieut. Col. Raymond F. Crist Jr., 36, husband of Mrs. Mary Devereux Crist, 3260 Gunston Rd., Alexandria, son of Mrs. Gene (c) Crist and the late Raymond Crist, 3025 Newark Ave. NW. (Wounded in August at Guam.)

First Lieut. Melvin W. Correll, 26, field artillery, husband of Mrs. Glenna I. Correll, 210 Maple Ave., Takoma Park. (Wounded in Belgium, December 29.)

Pfc. Rene G. Parker, 21, infantry, Third Army, son of Mrs. Margaret G. Parker, 1821 Summit Pl. NW. (Wounded December 19, Metz.)

Cpl. Osborne S. Belt, 23, fie'd artillery, Twenty-eighth Division, son of Mrs. Bertha V.

Pfc. F. L. Burch (Killed) Pvt. K. W. McCeney (Killed)

Sgt. T. W. Smith (Wounded) Lt. M. W. Correll (Wounded)

(Wounded December 9, Leyte.)

Cpl. Richard M. Hale, 31, Seventy-fifth Infantry Division, husband of Mrs. Elizabeth M. Hale, 605 North Irving St., Arlington. (Wounded December 31, Belgium.)

Sgt. Thomas W. Smith, 21, Third Army, son of Mr. and Mrs. Thomas W. Smith, 5436 Thirty-second St. NW. (Wounded February 3, Germany.)

Lieut. Granier Gives Life to Save Others

gagements and the first and second battles of the Philippines. One destroyer had been blasted from under him.

Before the Luzon invasion he was returned to the States for special training at the Anacostia Naval Training Station. He arrived here shortly before he learned of his father's death. He entered the Navy seven years ago, while studying in Washington. Arrangements are being completed for military rites at Arlington National Cemetery.

Private Barr, graduate and former football star at Central High School, entered the Army three years ago and went overseas in October 1943. He was employed in the map section at the War College before entering the service. Two brothers, Arthur C. and Allen Barr, are serving at sea with the Navy, and another, S/Sgt. Wilbur Barr, is at Camp Springs after serving three and a half years in Puerto Rico.

Returns To Action

Sergeant Blevins has returned to action after recovering from his injuries. He entered the service in July 1940, and served from November 1940 to June 1943, in Panama. He went overseas seven months ago.

Private Purey entered the Army in May 1942, and went overseas

Call REpublic 1234 for a Classified Ad-Taker

Many of TW's friends were wounded in WW II, including his good friend and first-year Citadel roommate Charlie Forrest. Charlie Forrest was from Johnston, South Carolina, and was in the 9th Infantry Division of the 47th Regiment. Forrest landed in Normandy on D-Day and relayed memories of fellow GIs drowning after coming off their landing crafts due to their heavy back-backs. His first injury occurred less than two weeks after his D-Day landing. As reported in the Anderson Independent in February 1989, Forrest recalled an incident with a fellow GI:

> Dead soldiers lay on the beach and we scrambled around them while ducking 88 mortar shells that burst overhead. After about 10 or 12 days fighting day and night we had moved away from the beach into the hedgerows; that was when a shell burst over us. We dived for the same trench but not in time—we were both hit by shrapnel. I called for a medic and as he ran toward us he was blown to bits.

After recuperating, Forrest returned to his division and, like TW, fought in the Battle of the Bulge. During the war, Forrest was wounded three times and received three purple hearts. Forrest was shot on two separate occasions in the back. To many people, getting hit in the back has a certain stigma attached to it. According to TW, however:

> *Charlie never seemed to mind. He always said "I knew when to get the hell out of there."*

In a letter to Forrest dated March 10, 1989, TW explained:

> *You may recall me telling you that when I learned that you had been wounded in action I was determined to avenge the matter. A short time after landing on Utah Beach however I began to have second thoughts. After my unit was hit by Germans in a fierce attack I began to wonder "what the hell did Charlie do to make those Germans so mad?"*

In addition to Graham Northrup and Charlie Forest, TW's grade school friend Alan Prosise was also wounded in Europe. Alan Prosise was a pilot in the Army Air Force and was shot down over Rhineland while flying his first mission in a P-51 Mustang fighter plane. TW recalls that TW and Prosise had scheduled a time to meet in Europe. TW showed up for the meeting, but Prosise did not. TW later learned that Prosise failed to show up because he ended up in a German prison camp after his plane was shot down. Dave Bell spoke with Alan Prosise about the incident:

> Prosise said that after his plane was hit, he could not get out, so he rolled the plane over on its back. He then ejected straight down and shot out so fast that he broke his shoulder when his parachute pulled.

TW remembers Prosise telling him what happened next:

> *Prosise jumped out of the plane and landed in what he described as "an unfortunate part of town." The Germans rushed him with guns drawn, yelling "Hände nach oben! " [Hands up!] He nearly lost his life when he was unable to find the German words for "my shoulder is broken, I cannot raise my arm."*

Prosise was taken as a German prisoner of war, and Dave Bell remembers Prosise telling of how he was lucky to have a German military escort, because the German civilians, who had been bombed repeatedly, wanted desperately to kill him and any other member of the U.S. Air Force. Prosise told TW what happened after he was brought to the prison. As TW recalls:

> *After a few days, the Germans took Prosise into a basement interrogation room. He said there were torture implements mounted on the wall. Prosise refused to tell them anything other than his name, rank and serial number. Sometime later, the Germans informed him that if he would not tell them about himself, the Germans would tell him. The Germans went on to tell Prosise where he grew up, that he played football at the University of Virginia and various other details of his life. He was totally surprised by this, and later learned that the Germans had researched his name through various newspapers.*

TW recalls that Prosise did not speak negatively about his German prison guards.

> *Prosise said the guards were elderly soldiers, veterans of WW I. He said they were always kind to him, and were just as hungry and ate the same food as the American prisoners. Toward the end of the war, Prosise woke up one morning and all the German guards were gone.*

Charlie Forrest, Graham Northrup and Alan Prosise each received purple hearts.

11. RACE TO THE RHINE; V-E DAY

"Apparently the Germans heard I was in O.C.S. and surrendered."

After recovering from trench foot and frostbite, TW returned to E-301 *"near Rhein-hausen, a town on the Rhine River,"* where TW recalls that there were *"patrols and rifle shooting but nothing like before."* During this period, the 94th Infantry Division captured Gusenburg, Reinsfeld, Mandern, Kell and Grimburg. TW recalls advancing on the town of Oggersheim on March 23, 1945, and the Division History notes that:

> Company E moved past a hospital and across an open park, taking a large bunker which was found to contain 1,800 civilians.

During the period March 13-24, 1945, the Division History notes that:

> The 94th Infantry Division with its attachments broke through the enemy lines east of the Saar River, overran all hostile resistance and actually spearheaded the advance of several American divisions over a hundred miles of German soil to the Rhine River. During this drive large amounts of enemy supplies and material were captured or destroyed. Elements of eighteen separate German divisions were encountered and the men of the 94th assisted materially in the annihilation of more than a few of these units. The Division took over two hundred towns and with the assistance of CCA of the 12th Armored Division captured the key city of Ludwigshafen. During this period, 13,434 German prisoners of war were captured.

Remembering this period, Leon Standifer of Company K, 301st Regiment noted:

> We were dog-tired but we kept going, crossed the river, took casualties and kept moving. British forces had a policy of trying to relieve troops who had been in combat for forty-eight hours. German generals used a longer rotation period, but even they were amazed at the way Patton drove us. (We were a bit surprised at him also.)

During the weeks leading up to reaching the Rhine River, General Patton wrote to his wife, Beatrice in a March 19, 1945, letter:

> The Third Army is really going to town today in the greatest operation we ever put on. . . WE ARE THE EIGHTH WONDER OF THE WORLD. And I had to beg, lie and steal to get started.

An earlier February 21, 1945 conversation between Major General Malony and Major General Walker expressed similar sentiments from the strong-willed General Patton:

> We are doing our damndest. We are doing this on a shoestring. I will tell you what George [Patton] told me. He said, "Johnny, you have done a wonderful job." The way he said 'me' he means you and the other fellow, but he said "and you done it without a goddamn bit of cooperation or support from anybody." That is pretty good coming from that fellow. That is what he said. You can tell your people that; that means something.

Major General Malony jokingly replied, "I got to have something; I can't walk."

General Patton had been referred to as a "military maverick" who defied convention, one example of which was noted by the Reverend Manning:

> Patton felt he had the world at his feet. He had thumbed his nose at Eisenhower, and his gamble had paid off. Now, as he received an urgent message from SHAEF urging him to bypass Trier because it would take four divisions to capture it, he radioed back, his triumph all too obvious: "Have taken Trier with two divisions (10th Armored and 94th Infantry). What do you want me to do, give it back?"

Despite their differences, Dwight Eisenhower later wrote in a General Order of Patton's "bold and brilliant leadership," noting that his "sound tactical knowledge, skillful, farsighted judgment, and masterful generalship contributed in the highest degree to the success of the Allied arms," noting also that Patton's Third Army was "a fighting force that is not excelled in effectiveness by any other of equal size in the world."

On March 21, Patton wrote in his diary that "I really believe this operation is one of the outstanding operations in the history of war." In fact, Hitler himself had predicted earlier that "no power in the world could penetrate Germany's western fortifications." The captured German chief of the Luftwaffe similarly described the American advance as "wholly incomprehensible," adding during interrogation that "we could not believe that these fortifications could be penetrated." Indeed, the Allied success was perhaps reminiscent of the American Revolutionary War victory at Trenton, after which General Washington observed "this is a glorious day for our country."

General Patton was deservedly proud, and a bit defiant, regarding the 94th Division's accomplishments. Upon successfully reaching the Rhine River, General Patton stopped to "take a piss in the Rhine," noting "I have been looking forward to this for a long time." On March 29, 1945, General Patton wrote to General Malony of the 94th Infantry Division:

> Please accept for yourself and extend to the officers and men of your command the sincere appreciation of all other members of the Third Army for the splendid work your Division has accomplished during its tour of duty with us. We appreciate what you have done, and we are sure that in your next assignment you will be equally successful.

TW notes that General Patton's men likewise appreciated his leadership, and TW recalls with pride that one day during the war, General Patton reviewed the 94th Division troops.

> *I was too far in the back to see him, but there was a lot of excitement around his stopping by to see us.*

While reviewing the troops of TW's 301st Regiment, Patton praised the 94th Infantry Division's accomplishments, referring to the division as his "Golden Nugget" and exclaiming:

> That is a beautiful and inspiring sight. You should be proud of them. The only criticism I have to offer the American soldier is that he doesn't realize how good he is. You're the best soldiers that ever walked in shoe leather, and don't you forget it."

Following the 94th Division's advance into Oggersheim and Ludwigshafen in March 1945, the Division History notes that TW's 301st Regiment advanced to Bobenheim-am-Berg, "while the remaining battalion of Colonel Hagerty's regiment closed at Leistadt." Afterwards, "the last elements had been relieved and for the first time since January 7, the 94th Infantry Division was out of contact with the enemy." From there, the "foot elements of the Division had moved to Bouzonville, on the French border, by truck and

General George S. Patton reviewing 94th troops. SC209589

While TW and the 94th Infantry Division continued to make significant advances through Germany in the Spring of 1945, U.S. troops invaded the Japanese island of Okinawa on April 1, 1945. Fierce Japanese resistance resulted in 35,000 American fatalities before the U.S. completed the capture of the island on June 21, 1945.

there boarded 40-and-8s for the remainder of the journey.... Immediately, the infantry elements moved to effect the relief of the 102nd Infantry Division. This was completed on the 3rd [of April]; the 94th was back in business," and "Colonel Hagerty's regiment and Colonel Johnson's took over the Division's new front line positions."

After driving to the Rhine River, the 94th Division had moved on to reach Krefeld, Germany, in April 1945 where it successfully contained the Ruhr pocket from German advances. While in the Krefeld area, the Division History notes:

> Patrol action across the Rhine continued and the artillery battalions of the Division actively engaged targets across the river. Despite the fact that observation was poor, interdictory fire, harassing fire and area target shooting inflicted extensive damage on German personnel and material. Some counter-battery fire was received but this was spotty and there were no large concentrations.

TW's friend Bob Bowden of the E-301 second platoon was taken prisoner on April 6, 1945, after crossing the Rhine River in a rowboat with an eight-man patrol. The men went to search what was believed to be an abandoned house on the other side of the river. Upon reaching the other side, Sergeant Bowden climbed up the steep bank toward the house and then heard shots fired, followed by yelling and splashing water in the vicinity where his men were waiting in the boat below. Separated from his men, he later tried to swim back across the river but turned back after realizing he could not survive the fast moving icy water. Bowden was captured and taken to a prison camp comprised of a barn surrounded by fencing with armed German guards and approximately 100 American, British and French prisoners. He later learned that five of his eight-man patrol had been killed. Bowden remained in the prison camp until April 16, 1945, when he was freed by the 78th Infantry Division. Like so many life and death events during WW II, he still thinks about the patrol sixty-five years later, and wonders "what I could have done differently."

While resuming military activities, the 94th Infantry Division also assisted with military police and government activities, including enforcing health regulations, managing civilians and liberated slave laborers, allocating food supplies, and closing schools to prevent further distribution of Nazi propaganda. The division history notes that "in the areas of the

On April 12, 1945, President Roosevelt died of a cerebral hemorrhage, just two and half months after being inaugurated to an unprecedented fourth term as President of the United States. On April 14, 1945, a funeral train carrying President Roosevelt's casket crossed the Potomac River and pulled into Union Station, where TW and Dave Bell had departed for the war nearly two years earlier. TW mourned the loss of the President who led the country for over half of TW's life, and the Division History notes that "the blow was doubly tragic in that the President did not live to see the victory which was so close and for which he had given so much." President Roosevelt was succeeded by his Vice President, Harry S. Truman, who understandably was overwhelmed by his new responsibilities, noting "I felt like the moon, the stars and all the planets had fallen on me." On April 28, 1945, Italian Dictator Benito Mussolini and his mistress were executed by Italian anti-fascists. The next day, their bodies were hung by the heels from lampposts in Milan.

301st and 302nd Infantry along the Rhine, there was the additional problem of keeping civilians from returning to the restricted area which extended westward five hundred yards from the river." Fortunately, "attempts at sabotage and subversive acts by German civilians were few and of a minor nature," although the Division History notes that "there was a constant quest for Nazi big shots, Gestapo agents and SS thugs." The 94th Division also helped manage thousands of displaced people from Russia, Poland, Ukraine, Italy, Lithuania, the Netherlands and Yugoslavia, which included preventing looting and managing those who "had old scores to settle with the Germans and did so at every opportunity."

At this point, Nazi resistance in Europe was reaching its final stages. The Ruhr pocket had been split and was yielding over 3,000 prisoners a day, eventually reaching 315,000 and including fifty-officers. From Krefeld, the 94th Division crossed the Rhine and moved to the Dusseldorf sector, where it handled similar duties as in Krefled, including "overall security, area control, salvage of cached and abandoned arms, equipment, ammunition and demolitions, and protection of Rhine bridges." The Division also "enforced military government regulations, curfew restrictions and travel prohibitions; apprehended prisoners of war; and located and reported abandoned enemy installations and material."

On April 29, 1945, TW's good friend David Bell and the 222nd Infantry Regiment of the 42nd Rainbow Division liberated the concentration camp at Dachau, Germany. In contrast to Alan Prosise's experience with German prison guards, the GIs of the Rainbow division discovered abused, starved and tortured prisoners and evidence of gruesome medical experiments. Located near Munich, Dachau was the first Nazi concentration camp located in Germany. Dave Bell remembered that with the Russians overrunning

1993 photo taken of entrance to Dachau by TW Smith, III.

Germany in the East, the Germans were transporting boxcars full of people by rail to Dachau. Upon arriving at the camp, Bell saw fifteen 40 x 8 boxcars full of dead bodies on the railroad outside the camp, all apparently gunned down as the doors were opened to disembark. Bell vividly remembers the scene.

> Each car was designed to hold eight horses or forty people, but there were far more than forty dead bodies in each car. The people were stacked in there like sardines. It was quite a scene for a twenty-year old to take in…. On the entire train, we only found one survivor amongst the bodies, and his picture was later taken with our division.

Bell remembers that some American GIs "went nuts" after seeing the horrors of Dachau and responded at the scene by shooting anyone in a German uniform. Other prison guards were killed by liberated prisoners, some of whom decapitated their former captors with the swing of a shovel. When asked about the concentration camp, Bell noted:

> I never went inside the camp walls. Three weeks earlier, half my platoon was killed or imprisoned. I just didn't want to see anymore dead or dying people. I had seen enough of that already. I also knew about diseases in the camps, and part of our job was to contain the prisoners from leaving the camp and infecting others in town. Another thing I'll never forget was the worst stench you could ever imagine.

Bell also remembers walking past the distinctive main gate to the camp and reading the daunting wrought iron sign with the words "Arbeit Macht Frei," meaning "work makes one free."

On the same day that Bell and his regiment liberated Dachau, German Dictator Adolf Hitler married his mistress Eva Braun and dictated his last will and political testament, declaring in closing that "Above all, I charge the leadership of the nation and their followers with the strict observance of the racial laws and with merciless resistance against the universal poisoners of all peoples, international Jewry." The following day, April 30, 1945, in an effort to avoid Mussolini's fate, Hitler and his new wife committed suicide in Hitler's bunker in Berlin as Soviet troops advanced through the city only a few blocks away. Braun died after swallowing cyanide. The sixty-five year old Hitler, who had become German Chancellor exactly twelve years and three months earlier, shot himself in the head with a Walther PPK. Seven days later, his Third Reich fell.

Although one of his best friend's units helped to liberate Dachau, and the Third Army liberated concentration camps at Ohrdruf and Buchenwald, TW did not see the concentration camps or related holocaust atrocities. TW read and heard much about the camps, which were so heinous that General Patton vomited at one site and could scarcely stand the stench. TW adds *"I'm glad I didn't see any of that. They were slaughtered."*

During this time, the Army sent TW to Officer Candidate School in Fontainebleau, France.

> *It seems that the Army had lost so many infantry second lieutenants that they started an Officer Candidate School at Fontainebleau, France, which is near Paris. The war was still going on. I was offered a chance to go to O.C.S. and accepted.*

Similar to his experience following frostbite and trench foot, TW learned that his replacement in the E Company of the 301st Regiment was killed soon after TW left for OCS. After noting with dismay that *"two of my successors were killed,"* TW speculated that *"if I hadn't decided to become an officer, I'd have been killed right then and there."*

While at OCS in Fontainebleau, TW and his fellow officer candidates were able to see Paris, where they posed for a group picture. From May 2, 1945, to June 28, 1945, TW completed "Officer Candidate Course Number Twenty Four." During that time he posed with two friends for a picture in Fontainebleau, France, and later received his certificate of completion.

Following OCS, TW was commissioned as a Second Lieutenant, Infantry, which would allow him to lead a rifle platoon. On June 4, 1945, TW received a congratulatory letter from Brigadier General E. J. Dawley of the Ground Force Reinforcement Command, European Theater of Operations. Addressed to Lieutenant Smith, the letter states that "you have

TW, back row under arrow.

TW, center

satisfied the authorities that be, that you are competent to undertake the job of Platoon leader of Infantry; there is probably no more exacting role in the Army for a junior officer." General Dawley offered TW many words of advice in the letter, including:

> If we are to have an Army in which the definition of a leader holds, "A leader is one who has followers," you must know and appreciate the power of example. As you require enlisted personnel to be punctilious, meticulous and correct in their observance of the requirements of military courtesy, you must be equally punctilious, meticulous and correct. As you require them to be correct in their attire, posture and cleanliness, you must be equally so, or better. The unshaven, long-haired person in any station or any walk in life, marks himself as a lout. There is no place in the military for louts.

General Dawley also advised TW to give orders "as you would your own, without a hint of apology, either in text or manner," and to always give and expect the highest standards and efforts, noting:

> [Regarding citations of valor], I am sure you will be struck with the fact that very often somebody, somewhere, has won with a remnant; that it has usually been that an individual has stuck, or has carried on or achieved the highest accomplishment with the greatest valor. Read what military history you will and you will find that behind or beneath every success, there was a remnant at some critical point, which made possible the big victory.

Upon returning from the war, TW framed General Dawley's letter, the message from which is consistent with Patton's proclamation that:

> Wars may be fought with weapons, but they are won by men. It is the spirit of the men who follow and of the man who leads that gains the victory.

TW still keeps the framed letter in his office.

Several days later in June, General Patton returned to the United States where he addressed a jubilant crowd estimated at more than a million people in Boston:

> My name is merely a hook to hang the honors on. This great ovation by Boston is not for Patton the general, but Patton as a symbol of the Third Army.

During the same month, TW celebrated his new commission with girls of the American Red Cross.

The Red Cross photo above shows GIs celebrating their officer commissions with Red Cross girls. TW is dancing with the girl on the left. The tagline below was published with the picture.

RED, WHITE AND HOT!

Straighten up and fly right! It's a GI jive session, Siegfried line style, slowed down by a soggy dance floor but otherwise in the groove. Smiling Red Cross girls help the boys forget the war for a moment.

Red Cross Photo

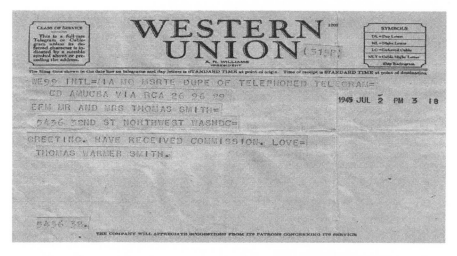

On July 2, 1945, TW sent his parents a Western Union telegram stating:

Greeting, Have received commission. Love Thomas Warner Smith

On July 8, 1945, TW's name and new rank were published in the Washington Star along with other newly promoted officers from the Washington, D.C., area, and the new 2nd Lieutenant posed for a picture (opposite page).

While in O.C.S., TW speculates that *"apparently the Germans heard I was in O.C.S. and surrendered."* Germany unconditionally surrendered to the Allied Forces on May 7, 1945. On May 8, 1945, Victory in Europe (V-E) Day celebrations took place throughout Europe and the United States.

The 94th Infantry Division had reason to celebrate, and General Malony's V-E Day message to his 94th Infantry Division troops noted:

> This is the day for which we have trained and fought for two and a half years. What it has cost us, you only well know.

The 94th Infantry Division started with over fifteen thousand men and paid a heavy price for this day. Following 209 combat days, the Division suffered 10,957 casualties, which included 1,087 killed in action, 45 non-battle deaths, 113 missing in action, 4,684 wounded in action, and 5,028 casualties from causes mainly including trench foot and frozen feet. The division's three infantry regiments (302nd, 376th, and TW's 301st) suffered the brunt of the casualties. With the same "unremitting courage and perseverance" that General Washington called for during the Revolutionary War, the 94th Infantry Division's accomplishments were significant, including the capture of thousands of acres from German forces and hundreds of cities and towns, as well as 26,638 German prisoners. General Malony's V-E Day message added "this Division has never failed in a mission, nor has it ever permanently lost one inch of ground to the enemy."

2nd Lieutenant TW (still wearing his Movado watch)

Described as a "hard-driving, unrelenting military machine," Patton's Third Army liberated territory in France, Germany, Luxembourg, Belgium, Czechoslovakia and Austria, including some twelve thousand towns and communities. The battles waged by General Patton's Third Army proved critical to the ultimate defeat of Adolf Hitler and his German forces. Describing the obstacles to this accomplishment, General Patton noted in a V-E Day speech that "you have captured more than three-quarters of a million Nazi soldiers and have killed or wounded at least half a million others." Speaking of his Third Army, Patton explained that "neither intolerable weather nor the best troops in the possession of the Germans were able to stop them nor prevent their supply." General Dwight Eisenhower likewise noted in May 1945 that the Third Army had "achieved

Daily Progress newspaper TW's parents saved from May 7, 1945

perfection in unification of air, ground, and naval power that will stand as a model in our time."

Despite these accomplishments, TW does not remember any special celebration, noting "*the war was not over; we were still fighting the Japanese.*" TW later read of President Truman's May 8, 1945, announcement expressing similar sentiments and explaining that "this is a solemn but glorious hour…. We must work to finish the war. Our victory is but half won…." Patton had already sent word to his superiors explaining "I should like to be considered for any type of combat command from a division up against the Japanese."

12. OFF TO JAPAN; V-J DAY

"We were nine days out of Antwerp Belgium when the A Bombs were dropped ending WW II."

TW was then sent to Antwerp, Belgium, where the Army was assembling a new regiment of veterans with combat infantry experience in preparation for the invasion of Japan. Meanwhile, General Patton, who made repeated politically incorrect public statements and was becoming increasingly outspoken in his opposition to Russia, was passed over for command in Japan. General Douglas MacArthur had no interest in Patton, who at this point was perceived by Eisenhower as an impulsive and explosive personality who was perhaps "mentally unbalanced."

Following preparations in Antwerp, TW and his new regiment then boarded a boat for the invasion of Japan. TW recalled the events in an August 17, 1999, letter to Doug Benson of E-301 as follows:

> *In August 1945, I was on a troop ship loaded with combat infantrymen. Our ultimate objective was the invasion of Japan. We were nine days out of Antwerp Belgium when the A Bombs were dropped ending WW II.*

By this point, President Truman had authorized the mobilization of over one million troops to attack Japan, including thirty divisions from Europe and the Pacific. Japan likewise had assembled over two million troops and was arming and training civilian men and women for combat. On July 16, 1945, four days after TW's twenty-second birthday, the United States tested the world's first atomic bomb in New Mexico, and the results were reported as "successful beyond the most optimistic expectations of anyone." Conceived in 1939, the top secret Manhattan Project grew to employ some 600,000 people and was so secret that Harry Truman only learned of its existence after he assumed the Presidency in April 1945. Two weeks after the successful testing, the USS Indianapolis delivered to Tinian Island air base the parts for the atomic bomb that would later be dropped on Hiroshima. On its return trip, the USS Indianapolis was sunk on July 30, 1945, by two torpedoes from a Japanese submarine, killing more than 800 sailors.

TW recalls traveling with full combat gear and thinking things were *"gonna get worse."* Truman had similar concerns and expressed his hope that "there was a possibility of preventing an Okinawa [where the U.S. suffered 35% casualties] from one end of Japan to the other." After nine days of travel, the canons on the ship began firing without warning, and men raced out to the deck, stumbling over each other and thinking they were engaging in combat. It was a celebration that Japan had surrendered. Like Germany's surrender, TW often jokes that *"Japanese intelligence must have learned I had received my commission and was on the way, and immediately surrendered."*

Japan's decision to surrender was an unprecedented action, which Emperor Hirohito described in his August 1945 broadcast to his Japanese people:

> But now the war has lasted for nearly four years. Despite the best that has been done by everyone— the gallant fighting of our military and naval forces, the diligence and assiduity of our servants of the State and the devoted service of our 100 million people— the war situation has developed not necessarily to Japan's advantage, while trends of the world have all turned against her interest. . . . Should we continue to fight, it would not only result in an ultimate collapse and obliteration of the Japanese nation, but also it would lead to the total extinction of human civilization.

TW knew the Japanese were brutal and relentless opponents, fighting to the death and refusing to surrender, which they considered dishonorable. While many criticized the United States for using atomic weapons, TW and his fellow GIs supported the decision.

Japan surrendered on August 14, 1945. Formal surrender ceremonies took place on September 2, 1945; six years and one day after the war began. The Japanese surrender was precipitated by the United States' dropping of atomic bombs on the Japanese cities of Hiroshima and Nagasaki. The U.S. B-29 named the Enola Gay dropped the "Little Boy" atomic bomb on Hiroshima on August 6, 1945, killing approximately 140,000 people. Following the bombing of Hiroshima, President Truman announced that "[i]f they do not now accept our terms they may expect a rain of ruin from the air, the like of which has never been seen on this earth." The U.S. B-29 named Bock's Car dropped the "Fat Man" atomic bomb on Nagasaki on August 9, 1945, killing approximately 70,000 people.

Following the bombing, President Truman explained to the American people:

> Having found the bomb we have used it. We have used it against those who attacked us without warning at Pearl Harbor, against those who have starved and beaten and executed American prisoners of war, against those who have abandoned all pretense of obeying international laws of warfare. We have used it in order to shorten the agony of war, in order to save the lives of thousands and thousands of young Americans. We shall continue to use it until we completely destroy Japan's power to make war. Only a Japanese surrender will stop us.

Regarding the decision to use the bomb, U.S. Major General Curtis LeMay bluntly confirmed the reality of the situation: "I'll tell what war is about…. You've got to kill people, and when you've killed enough, they stop fighting." Similarly expressing no remorse, Morris Jeppson, who passed away in March 2010 and was one of two weaponeers who armed the Little Boy bomb on board the Enola Gay, told a reporter that he had no regrets about the bombing and that his wife's car bore the bumper sticker "If there hadn't been a Pearl Harbor, there wouldn't have been a Hiroshima."

TW and his fellow 94th Infantry division veterans continue to support the decision to use the atomic bombs, believing it was in the best interest of the United States and world peace and that their lives depended on it.

> *Prior to these bombings, there were predictions of over one million GI casualties in the invasion of Japan. Knowing how fiercely the Japanese would have defended their beaches behind barricades and in foxholes, and how many GIs were killed just fighting the Japanese on small islands, I've always thought that President Truman's decision to drop the atomic bombs saved my life, and countless others.*

Several months after the bombing, President Truman, who kept a sign on his desk reading "the buck stops here," expressed similar sentiments, noting "[i]t occurred to me that a quarter of a million of the flower of our young manhood were worth a couple of Japanese cities, and I still think they were and are." British Prime Minister Winston Churchill likewise noted that "there was unanimous, automatic, unquestioned agreement around our table."

Following Japan's surrender, TW traveled by boat to New York. Unlike his trip to Europe as a private on the Queen Elizabeth where he was "triple bunked" with two other GIs and ate the same thing every day, TW's trip home as an officer was much more comfortable. TW had his own bed, shared a room with a fellow officer, and had his choice of menu items for meals. A newspaper article announced the arrival of Washington area veterans, including TW, whose name is listed at the bottom of the first column.

Sixty Area Veterans Arrive At New York by Saturday

NEW YORK PORT OF EMBARKATION, Aug. 15. Twenty-six Washington area veterans of the European war are scheduled to arrive here tomorrow with 34 more District men due to arrive Saturday. The men are part of a contingent returning on 10 small transports.

Those arriving tomorrow include:

Lt. E. Paton Albert, [...] SE.; Lt. Helm Meredith, Riverdale; [...] Henry N. Bond jr., 5012 Quarles St. NE.; Lt. H. Barge Robert jr., Alexandria; Lt. Charles A. Fuller jr., 5017 Lowell St. NW.; Lt. Thomas W. Smith, 5436 Thirty-second St. NW.; Pfc. Ralph F. Baxter, 182 Thirty-fifth St. NE.; Sgt.

Rd., Arlington; Pfc. Arnold Arnold, N. Military Rd., Arlington; Cpl. Aubrey F. Wright, 607 Rittenhouse St. NW.; Pfc. Ralph Cleveland, 20 Anacostia Rd. SE.; Pfc. Andrew H. Kirkpatrick, W. Underwood St., Chevy Chase; Pfc. Richard Lang, Strathmore St., Chevy Chase, Md.; Pfc. Harry Marcey, Marcey Rd., Arlington.

Pvt. Johnnie O. Edwards, Arcola Ave., Silver Spring; Pv. Joseph E. Wade, 1362 B St. SE.; Lt. Col. Louis L. Ingram, MacArthur St., Alexandria; Lt. Carl R. Keeler, 1359 Pennsylvania Ave. SE.; Pfc. Allen Copeland, 2943 Park Rd. NW.; Pfc. Thomas L. Pettit jr., 602 Atlantic St. SE.; Pvt. John H. Wright, 482 H St. SW.; S/Sgt James A. Dimery, 1346 Twenty-eighth St. NW.; T/4 Thomas Harris, 1911 L St. NW.; T/4 Alfred H. Hill, Larch Ave., Takoma Park; T/5 Marshall L. Beverly, 1051 Forty-eighth Pl. NW.; Pfc. Horace W. Buggs, 207 Second St. NE.; Pvt. Andrew Ashton, 1704 First St. NW.; Pvt. Bernard Frederick, 1232 R St. NE.

During this period, General Patton was discussing the need for the United States to attack Russia. He became increasingly volatile, perhaps also falling victim to certain radical members of the press, and on September 28, 1945, Eisenhower made the difficult decision to relieve Patton of command of his beloved Third Army. During Patton's farewell speech a week later, his men sang "For He's a Jolly Good Fellow," and Patton explained that "All good things must come to an end. The best thing that has ever happened to me thus far is the honor and privilege of having commanded the Third Army." On December 9, 1945, General Patton was severely injured in a car accident in Mannheim, Germany, while on route to a hunting trip. Although his driver and another passenger were uninjured, Patton was paralyzed from the neck down, after which he exclaimed "this is a helluva way to die." Patton died on December 21, 1945, at sixty years of age. One month earlier, the Nuremberg war trials commenced in Nuremberg, Germany, during which Nazi political and military leaders were tried for war crimes. In the first trial, half of the infamous twenty-four defendants were given the death sentence and killed by hanging in 1946. In a series of trials lasting many years, hundreds more would later be tried and found guilty of war crimes, often leading to imprisonment or execution. The Allies similarly brought an estimated 5,000 Japanese war criminals to trial, with as many as 900 condemned to execution and thousands more sentenced to life in prison.

Pictures of 2nd Lieutenant TW at Fort McClellan

Upon arriving in New York, TW boarded a train to Camp Gordon in Georgia.

> *When I went to Camp Gordon, they had no orders for me. I waited around Camp Gordon for several weeks.*

TW was told he could leave and just needed to check in every couple days until his orders arrived. TW hitchhiked around the South for a couple weeks visiting friends. He also visited Charlie Forrest's parents and then went to see Charlie Forrest who was still in a hospital in South Carolina recovering from WW II wounds.

After several weeks, TW recalls that he *"finally received orders to go to Fort McClellan, Alabama, a training center. There, I became an instructor of troops for the army of occupation."*

During the period of his service back in the states, TW's qualification records describe his responsibilities as follows:

> Officer was assigned to 2nd Infantry Training Regiment, Fort McClellan, Alabama, as a platoon officer. Officer supervised and administered groups of infantry trainees averaging 50 men. Responsibilities included supervision and direction of training, supply and morale and discipline of the unit. For a period of six weeks officer was assigned to the 1st Training Regiment, Camp Gordon,

Georgia. Duties included responsibility and accountability for all company property, supplies and equipment and for the proper handling of property, supply and equipment records during deactivation procedures.

TW was later sent to the Army separation center at Camp Meade Maryland, and honorably discharged on May 5, 1946 at 22 years of age. Upon returning from the war, TW posed for the following pictures, which include a relieved and grateful mother, whose smile is in stark contrast to her expression at Union Station several years earlier.

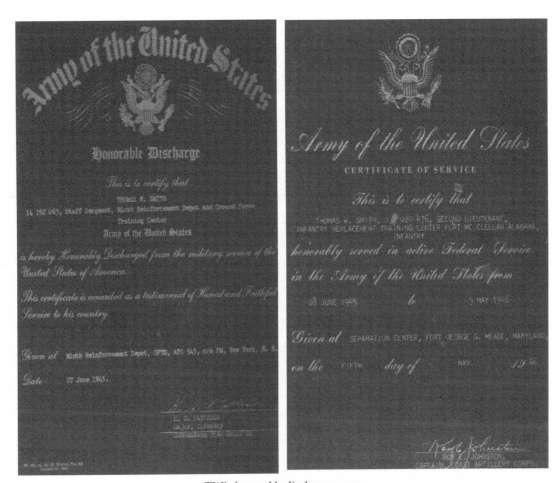

TW's honorable discharge papers

13. WW II MEDALS

"So I put it in my pocket and thought it'd make a good souvenir.
Then I told him 'Danke schön'."

Photographs from Division History of 94th Division taking prisoners in Serrig and Beuren

While having lunch together in June 2009, TW's friend Dave Bell explained that GIs used to joke that:

    Russians fought to protect their homeland,
    Germans fought for medals, and
    Americans fought for souvenirs.

Demonstrating some basis for the latter two statements, TW recalls obtaining a few souvenirs during the Battle of the Bulge while escorting German prisoners at gunpoint back to the battalion. While doing so, TW confiscated two German iron crosses and a number of medals from the prisoners he escorted. TW recalls that:

> As I was turning over one of the German prisoners, I saw something hanging on his jacket. So I put it in my pocket and thought it'd make a good souvenir. Then I told him "Danke schön."

Iron Cross

Close Combat Clasp

Deutschland Erwache Pin

The Wound Badge

Tank Battle Badge

Medal for the Winter
Campaign in Russia 1941-42

TW keeps the Iron Cross and medals, pictures of which are shown above, mounted in a frame hanging over his desk.

The Iron Cross was the best known of all German medals. First instituted in 1813 by Friedrich-Wilhelm III, there were eight classes of the Iron Cross by the end of WW II. The Iron Cross is sometimes referred to as the Knight's Cross. Many World War I veterans wore the Iron Cross on their SS uniforms, and Adolf Hitler received two Iron Crosses during his WW I service. As apparent on TW's WW II issue medal above, the WW II medal is distinguished from the WW I medal by the swastika in the center and the "1939" at the bottom. In contrast, the WW I iron cross contained an Imperial Crown.

The Wound Badge was awarded in three classes: black (for one or two wounds), silver (for three or four wounds), and gold (for five or more wounds). The silver could be awarded for loss of an eye, foot, hand, or deafness. The gold could be awarded for disablement or blindness. Adolf Hitler received a Wound Badge in WW I.

The Close Combat Clasp is a German military award instituted on November 25, 1942, for achievement in hand-to-hand fighting in close quarters. It was worn above the upper left uniform pocket and consisted of the national emblem surmounting a crossed bayonet and hand grenade. The Close Combat Clasp was awarded in three grades: bronze, silver, and gold for 15, 30, and 50 days respectively of engagement in close combat.

The Tank Battle badge was issued in silver for tank crews, and in bronze for "Panzer-Grenadier" and other armored fighting vehicle personnel.

The Medal for the Winter Campaign was issued to participants in the winter campaign in Russia during 1941-1942.

The Deutschland Erwache (Germany Awake) Pin is also known as the Nazi German Enamel Badge.

SS Sleeve Brassard

While escorting another German prisoner, TW obtained an armband and patch, shown above, which he keeps in a photo album in his office. SS men typically wore a swastika armband on their upper left sleeve. The Schutzstaffel (German for "Protective Echelon"), abbreviated "SS" served as the Nazi Party's "Shield Squadron." Built upon the Nazi racial ideology, the SS, under Heinrich Himmler's command, formed an order of men claimed to be superior in racial purity and abilities to other Germans and national groups, a model for the Nazi vision of a master race. Remembering the "SS" shield squadron, TW notes:

> *They were the worst ones of all.*

In addition to German medals TW obtained from German prisoners during the war, he received U.S. medals as a result of his service during WW II. TW received (bottom row, left to right, opposite page) the World War II Victory Medal; European-African-Middle Eastern Service Medal with four Battle stars for participation in Northern France, the Rhineland, the Ardennes and Central Europe Campaigns; Bronze Star Medal; American Campaign Medal; and Army Good Conduct Medal. TW received the Combat Infantry Man's Badge, (center with rifle, opposite page) which recognizes that TW was "personally present and under hostile fire while serving in an assigned infantry or special forces primary duty, in a unit actively engaged in ground combat with the enemy." TW received the Bronze Star Medal for "meritorious achievement in ground operations against the enemy on or about 1 October 1944 in Europe." The Bronze Star Medal is awarded to a person who "distinguished himself or herself by heroic or meritorious achievement or service, not involving participation in aerial flight, in connection with military operations against an armed enemy."

Asked why he received the Bronze Star, TW responded matter-of-factly *"I have no idea."*

TW's WW II tags, pins, ID, patch and medals

14. D.C. NEIGHBORHOOD FRIENDS

"A casualty very close to home."

5436 32nd Street *(TW)*	*5475 Nebraska Ave.* *(John Beall)*	*5453 Nebraska Ave.* *(Paul Dietrick)*	*5429 Nebraska Ave.* *(Harold Moynelo, Jr.)*

Many of TW's friends and neighbors fought in WW II, including three neighborhood boys who lived just a few houses away from TW on Nebraska Avenue. Nebraska Avenue ran diagonally directly behind TW's home on 32nd Street in Northwest Washington, D.C. Illustrating the vast scope of WW II, three boyhood friends of TW living within just a few houses of TW's home, were killed in widely differing regions of the war, including Tunisia, the Alps and the Pacific Ocean.

Captain John P. Beall *(KIA, April 1943, Tunisia)*

TW's friend John P. Beall lived at 5475 Nebraska Avenue, about eight houses down from TW's home. John Beall graduated from Georgetown University with honors in 1941 and was in the ROTC. Georgetown University's ROTC website notes the following about John Beall:

> WW II, more than any other war, took the highest toll on Georgetown's ranks. 171 were lost, including John Paul Beall [who] was the honor graduate of the Infantry ROTC in 1941. He became a Captain, the youngest Company Commander in the 9th Division. He participated in the U.S. coastal invasion of Algeria and was killed in action in Tunisia, 25 April 1943.

Beall was one of over 2,700 Americans killed in the Allied victory during the North African campaign. His 9th Division was part of the II Corps commanded by General Patton during the Spring of 1943, during which time Patton declared "if we are not victorious, let no one come back alive." TW had enlisted in the Army by this time but was still at home when Mrs. Beall came over to TW's house to tell TW's mother of the news of her son John's death.

> *My mother was visiting with Dave Bell's mom at our house. The doorbell rang and Mrs. Beall was at the door crying. She was holding the telegram from the Army notifying her of John's death in North Africa. All three women were distraught. This was a casualty very close to home for my mother and Mrs. Bell as well. Dave Bell and I were preparing to leave for the war at that time.*

The Bealls later sold their home at 5475 Nebraska Avenue to Ken Delavigne, an FBI agent who worked years later with TW. Ken Delavigne's wife, Mary Delavigne, also worked at the FBI with TW. In 2011, Mary Delavigne still lived at 5475 Nebraska Avenue and remained in touch with TW and his wife Janet.

First Lieutenant Paul A. Dietrick *(KIA, November 1944, the Alps)*

TW's friend Paul A. Dietrick lived at 5453 Nebraska Avenue, which was almost directly behind TW's house. Paul Dietrick was a First Lieutenant in the Air Force and served as an airplane navigator. On November 15, 1944, while TW was fighting in Brittany, Paul Dietrick was one of 11 crew members of the 765th Bomb Squad whose plane disappeared while on a mission to bomb a target in Innsbruck, Germany. Four planes deployed for the mission but only three planes returned. The missing air crew report filed three days later indicates that the plane disappeared "somewhere in the Alps." The report noted that there were snow showers in the target area and that the cause of the loss was "believed due to bad weather conditions."

Ensign Harold C. Moynelo, Jr. *(KIA, August 1945, Pacific Ocean)*

TW's friend Harold C. Moynelo, Jr., lived at 5429 Nebraska Avenue, which was about four houses away from TW's home. Harold Moynelo attended the U.S. Naval Academy and was commissioned as an Ensign before being assigned to the USS Indianapolis. While TW was preparing to depart for the invasion of Japan, the Indianapolis delivered top secret components of the atomic bomb codenamed "Little Boy" to Tinian Island Air Base. On its return trip, the Indianapolis was attacked at about midnight on July 30, 1945, by a Japanese submarine that saw the heavy cruiser under the moonlight about ten miles away. After being hit by two Japanese torpedoes, the Indianapolis sank in less than 12 minutes. Of the crew of 1,196 men, approximately 300 died from the initial explosion.

Over 500 sailors, including Harold Moynelo, drowned or died from exposure, dehydration or shark attacks as they floated for up to five days in the shark infested waters of the Philippine Sea waiting to be rescued. On August 6, 1945, the B-29 plane named the Enola Gay left Tinian Air Base for Hiroshima, along with the Little Boy atomic bomb containing the message "Greetings to the Emperor from the men of the Indianapolis."

TW recalls his discussions with Harold Moynelo's father after the war:

> *Following the end of the war, I was home visiting my parents when Harold Moynelo's father, who worked at Lansburg Department store, asked me for a ride to the Navy Yard to attend a hearing on the sinking of the Indianapolis. While at the Navy Yard, Mr. Moynelo and I met the Captain of the Indianapolis. The Captain came over and shook Mr. Moynelo's hand and then told us that after the Indianapolis was hit, he saw Ensign Moynelo in the water hanging onto debris and holding hands with other sailors floating in the water.*

That was TW's only first-hand account of his friend Harold Moynelo's final days. TW subsequently has read other accounts indicating that Ensign Moynelo was floating as late as day four with a group of other sailors and that he was looking out for other stray sailors to bring into the group. Dr. Lewis L. Haynes, the Chief Medical Officer on the Indianapolis, floated with Moynelo and a group of 400 other men in the water waiting to be rescued. When Dr. Haynes was finally picked up on August 3, 1945, only 96 men from this group were still alive. Shortly before his death in 2001, Dr. Haynes was interviewed for a Military History Channel documentary, during which he referenced TW's friend Harold Moynelo:

> People held me up, and I held others up. You had to stay together to stay alive. Captain Parks, for example, took off his jacket a couple of times and gave it to men. He worked, both he and Moynelo, keeping our group together, to the point where they died of exhaustion.

Some 880 men from the Indianapolis died in the South Pacific, and 316 men survived the five-day ordeal, including the ship's captain, Charles Butler McVay, III. At the November 1945 hearing at the Navy Yard, Captain McVay was court-martialed and demoted for failing to zigzag his ship to avoid enemy fire. TW remembers that:

> *Mr. Moynelo was not bitter toward Captain McVay when we met him at the Navy Yard hearing. We also met the commander of the Japanese submarine at the hearing. I understand he told them that he would have hit the Indianapolis even if it had zigzagged.*

Dr. Lewis Haynes also testified at the hearing, and later remembered the court-martial decision during the Military History Channel interview:

As a group, we all thought this was terrible; that McVay should not be court-martialed. This was just terrible.

Captain McVay committed suicide in 1968 by shooting himself with his navy service revolver while clutching a toy soldier in his hand. Captain McVay was exonerated by Congress and President Clinton in 2000 with a resolution that declared that "the American people should now recognize Captain McVay's lack of culpability for the tragic loss of the USS Indianapolis and the lives of the men who died."

In addition to TW's friends on Nebraska Avenue, TW remembers another friend who lived off Connecticut Avenue. TW recalls that his friend survived WW II and then decided to stay in the Army reserves. *"Years later his unit got called up to Korea and he was killed in action."*

In 1967, TW moved to 5918 Kimble Court in Falls Church, Virginia, where he and Janet raised their family and have lived for more than forty-five years. Four of his neighbors on Kimble Court fought in WW II (George Gasparis, William Nutt, John Schneider, and Col. Alfred Tillmann) and one served in the Women's Auxiliary Corps (Bessie Nutt). Although now deceased, each of these neighbors were close friends of TW and his family, and TW remains in touch with their children.

15. GI BILL AND THE FBI

"Like General Patton, Director Hoover had strong opinions about things."

Unlike many other countries, WW II had many positive impacts on the United States, and the country was more productive industrially following WW II than the rest of the world combined. In addition to its effect on the United States, the war also had a lasting influence on TW. Upon returning home from the war, TW along with fellow GIs Graham Northrup, Bill Bird and Thomas Hopper, attended George Washington University. There TW received a Bachelor of Arts degree in 1948 and a Law degree in 1949. TW's education at George Washington was funded by the GI Bill of Rights, commonly known as the "GI Bill", which Congress adopted in part in response to the efforts of the WW I Bonus Marchers that TW watched with his father in 1932.[7] Following graduation from George Washington, TW briefly practiced law and worked for the General Accounting Office. During this period, TW remained in the Army Reserves and advanced to the rank of First Lieutenant in the U.S. Army Transportation Corps on May 18, 1950.

TW's Army training and marksmanship expertise may also have influenced his permanent career choice. Having earlier progressed in law enforcement from KP (Kitchen Police) to MP (Military Police), TW decided to join the FBI (Federal Bureau of Investigation), which had a long track record of working cooperatively with the armed forces. TW joined the FBI in 1950 as a Special Agent at a starting salary of $5,000 per year.

Created in 1908 under President Theodore Roosevelt, the FBI is an intelligence agency and national security organization for the United States, operating with a motto of "Fidelity, Bravery, Integrity." Although already well trained with firearms, TW went

---

7 Following in his father's footsteps, TW's son Jefferson Thompson Smith obtained an MBA degree from George Washington University, funded by a scholarship from the Scottish Rite of Freemasonry. Although TW never pursued engineering past his ASTP Basic Engineering course at the University of Florida, his son Thomas Warner Smith, III, received undergraduate and graduate degrees in civil engineering from the University of Virginia.

TW's 1946 Second Lieutenant, Infantry and 1950 1st Lieutenant, Transportation Corps papers

TW (right) loading his revolver
at Quantico

TW (right) displaying target at Quantico

John Meyer, TW's father-in-law

*Janet and TW's wedding, St. Mathew's
Cathedral, February 17, 1962*

through a rigorous training program and was issued the FBI revolver that he carried to work each day, concealed in a shoulder holster under his dark suit, which always included a white shirt and a tie, topped with a Fedora hat. He also attended monthly firearms training at the FBI's shooting range in Quantico, Virginia.

With increasing FBI travel and work responsibilities, TW decided to officially end what had been a decade of military service, and he was honorably discharged from the U.S. Army Reserves on April 1, 1953.

In the late 1950s, TW met Janet Meyer on a Saturday night at the Officers Club in Washington, D.C. Janet moved to the D.C. area in 1952 from her hometown of Melrose, Minnesota. Like TW's father, Janet's father, John L. Meyer (above), served in Europe in WW I and was the victim of mustard gas attacks. Her brother Donald Meyer served in WW II in the South Pacific.

TW and Janet fell in love and were married on February 17, 1962, at St. Mathew's Cathedral in Washington, D.C. (above). TW was 39 years old when he married Janet and the couple quickly embarked on a new life together, first at the State House at DuPont Circle, and later in Northern Virginia where they raised five children.

TW worked at the FBI under the leadership of longtime Director J. Edgar Hoover. Like TW, J. Edgar Hoover was born in the District of Columbia and obtained a law degree from George Washington University. Like Tom Sr., Director Hoover was a devoted Free-mason. Director Hoover was a strict disciplinarian and a demanding leader who became director of the predecessor Bureau of Investigation in 1924, accepting only under the condition that the Bureau would be "free from politics." The Bureau of Investigation became the FBI under President Franklin Roosevelt. During WW II, Director Hoover led the FBI in running a foreign intelligence service in the Western Hemisphere under a 1939 directive from President Roosevelt, which continues to this day to define FBI authority relating to "espionage, counterespionage, sabotage, subversive activities, and related matters." While the word "subversive" was not well-defined, President Roosevelt concurred with Director Hoover's interpretation that intelligence efforts included investigation of "fascisti" and "nazi" activities. The FBI proved adept at catching attempted saboteurs, and President Truman, reflecting years later on the service of the FBI and other security agencies during WW II, wrote in his memoirs that:

> The country had reason to be proud of and have confidence in our security agencies. They had kept us almost totally free of sabotage and espionage during World War II.

Director Hoover continued as Director of the FBI until his death in 1972. During his forty-eight year tenure as Director, J. Edgar Hoover served under eight different Presidents. Reflecting on Director Hoover's leadership, TW recalls that *"Director Hoover and General Patton were cut from the same cloth."* He also chuckles while adding that *"I had three big bosses in life: George S. Patton, J. Edgar Hoover, and Janet M. Smith."*

TW's 1950 work files contain pages of rules promulgated by the Director, including:
- An agent must keep his affairs on a sound basis and not embarrass the Bureau.
- NEVER represent yourself to be an employee of another agency, but you can be someone else such as an insurance salesman.
- Read files from the bottom up.
- Untyped material in an office for over seven days is intolerable.
- All criticism of the Bureau should be reported.
- NO CONTACT WITH OFFICIALS OF CBS WITHOUT THE PERMISSION OF THE BUREAU.

Director Hoover made clear his expectations, and retired agent Joe Purvis later recalled additional rules:
- You can expect some mistakes to be made—certainly you can. You can excuse one or two, but only if they are mistakes of the head, not of the heart.
- Do your job with a strong hand, but be fair. Always be fair. Be firm. Never be arbitrary and never be arrogant, and never let anyone use you as a crutch.
- Don't court popularity. This destroys men.
- Don't cut corners and don't let someone else carry your load.
- Never be concerned over what other people think of you as long as your conscience is clear and you know you have been fair and decent.

TW (second from right) and Director Hoover (middle) along with five other Special Agents
photographed in 1955 after the six agents were admitted to the U.S. Supreme Court Bar.

Remembering the FBI handbook sixty years later, TW still sings a song he enjoyed with his fellow agents:

> *Hoover loves me yes I know, because the handbook tells me so,*
> *what a friend we have in Hoover!*

J. Edgar Hoover was an important figure in Washington, and TW recalls being assigned to a team that would transport the Director to a government hideaway in the event of a national emergency. The secure bunker, known as Mount Weather, is located in Virginia's Blue Ridge Mountains about fifty miles outside Washington, D.C.

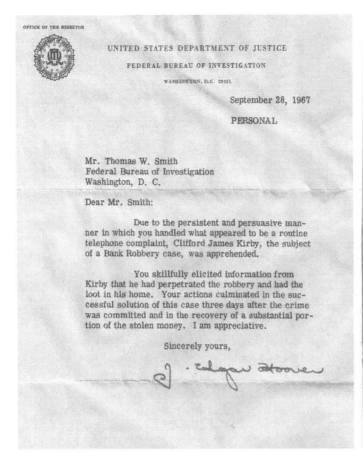

FBI Arrests Suspect in Bank Holdup

A Prince Georges County taxi driver was arrested by Federal Bureau of Investigation agents yesterday on charges of robbing a Sandston, Va., bank of $11,457 last week.

Rowland C. Halstead, special agent in charge of the FBI's Richmond bureau, said that Clifford Kirby, 27, of the 5500 block of 2nd Street, Temple Hills, Md., surrendered to agents at his home.

He was released on $10,000 bond pending appearance at a preliminary hearing next Monday before a U.S. Commissioner in Upper Marlboro, Md.

A man carrying three sticks of dynamite entered the Sandston branch of the Bank of Virginia at 9:30 a.m. last Wednesday. After threatening employes with the explosives, which were attached to two batteries, he escaped with the money.

We did practice runs every so often, but the plans only included my dropping Director Hoover off at the bunker. They never told me what to do after I dropped him off!

Fortunately, no national emergencies followed and TW never had to implement his well-practiced plans.

Like General Patton, Director Hoover respected his Special Agents, as reflected in congratulatory letters he sent to TW on the birth of his children and in the above 1967 "personal" letter he sent TW. The letter relates to TW's efforts to apprehend a taxi driver who robbed a Virginia bank. Some of the details of the incident are reflected in the above newspaper article, which TW recalls did not mention TW's name in order to protect his identity.

Director Hoover and his agents had a mutual respect for one another and TW enjoyed multiple opportunities to meet with him. Less than eight months prior to J. Edgar Hoover's death, the director autographed a picture "To Mr. and Mrs. Thomas Smith,

Best Wishes, J. Edgar Hoover, 9-12-71." The framed picture hangs in TW's office.

Director Hoover died on May 2, 1972, after which Congress passed a resolution authorizing his body to lie in state in the Capitol Rotunda. TW recalls attending Hoover's funeral and being assigned to transport a number of dignitaries to the service. In his eulogy, Chief Justice Warren spoke of Hoover's "unyielding integrity," noting further that "he was a patriot in the old-fashioned sense of those who love their country and its ideals and history." In a memorial service two days later, Brigadier General Eugene Lynch noted of Hoover:

> He was more than a dedicated servant of his nation. He was a soldier's soldier. In the darkest hours of WW II, while our Armed Forces fought on the far-flung battlefields of the world, he and his small vanguard protected our flanks and rear. And it was he and his small group of dedicated workers who have lived in the breach without rest so that others may live the life which our founding fathers envisioned.

TW and his FBI friends continue to hold great respect for Director Hoover and are somewhat "old school" when it comes to the FBI. Writing in a January 14, 1994, letter to TW, another FBI retiree and friend, Bill Turner, wrote:

> From all of the accounts that I read in the press and hear on TV I don't think I would recognize anything about the Bureau anymore, and I don't think Mr. Hoover would either. I suppose some of the changes have been for the better, but I find them hard to accept. I'm sort of like the old fellow who was asked on his hundredth birthday if he had seen a lot of changes. He replied that he had and had been against every one of them.

TW looks fondly back on his days at the FBI and takes satisfaction in the Bureau's accomplishments. Asked what he did at the FBI, TW responds by unknowingly quoting President Roosevelt's 1939 directive to Hoover:

> *I investigated espionage, counterespionage, sabotage, subversive activities, as well as crimes against the government, and illegal transportation of stolen property.*

TW carried a pistol to work each day and recalls his commute to work one day in the District of Columbia.

While sitting in my car at a light, a "gentleman" opened the car door and jumped into the car, apparently seeking money. He was surprised to find my gun pointed at him, after which he left faster than he came.

TW recalls a number of other times being assigned to follow suspected criminals. In one instance, the suspect knew he was being followed but did not know by whom. While on the subway, the suspect was so nervous that he grabbed the guy next to TW and accused him of following him. TW laughs, noting that *"he never did figure out that I was following him."* In another instance, TW was following a suspect who apparently also was having marital issues and figured out that he was being followed. TW recalls *"he came up to me and said he would pay me twice the amount his wife was paying me if I stopped following him."*

TW also laughs when remembering one woman's reaction when he presented his FBI special agent badge while on assignment. *"She looked at my badge and asked 'what is so special about you?'"* He also recalls going into a bar in NYC looking for an escaped prisoner and presenting the bartender his badge. *"The bartender looked at my badge and said 'mean looking guy, what did he do?'"*

TW recalls another incident in New York, this time with a New York police officer:

Another time when I was working in New York, I came up to a NY cop and asked him "Where's Amelia alley." He said see that little path down there, it goes off to the right, that's Amelia alley. But as I'm walking down there he said, "but they tell me don't dare go down there." So you know what? Recognizing that a NY cop would not go down there, I decided there was nobody there. . . . I'd still be down there if I had gone.

Another incident that TW recalls from when he was working on the docks in New York City involved efforts to obtain information on organized crime in the area. As was often the case, nobody wanted to talk to the FBI.

I knew one man had information, but he was reluctant to talk to a lawman, and everyone on the docks knew I was an agent. So when I went down to the docks, I made a special point of saying hi to this individual and loudly asking how he and his family were doing, mentioning some of them by name. After a few days of this, he quietly pulled me aside, gave me the information I needed, and asked me to stop talking to him because the locals were starting to think he was a rat.

On a more serious note, TW tells another FBI story, which like WW II, demonstrates again the chance circumstances of life and another fatal encounter with guns:

> *I remember once receiving a call over the radio about a federal prisoner down near Quantico that had escaped earlier in a prison yard truck. I later received an address for the escaped prisoner's wife in Anacostia. When I got there, several other agents were around, and there were two guys on the ground that had been shot dead. We knocked the door down, and carefully went in, but the convict had escaped out a window near a tree. We never found his wife. I then learned that the two guys on the ground were Woodriffe and Palmisano, two agents who occupied the office next to mine. They had been in the same car and just got there before I did. They had knocked on the door, and apparently the guy opened the door and shot and killed them both. The sad thing about it, Woodriffe was engaged to be married, and there's all kinds of sadness in addition to both of them being killed. Both men were in their twenties. We spent the rest of the day looking for him in that area and I think the fugitive was later found in an attic of a house. I don't know what they did to him. I hope they didn't give him a pardon.*

The FBI's Washington Field Office history account describes the event as follows:

> On January 8, 1969, tragedy struck the Washington Field Office when Special Agents Edwin R. Woodriffe (right) and Anthony Palmisano (left) were shot and killed by escaped federal prisoner Billie Austin Bryant. The agents had just entered a Southeast Washington apartment building where Bryant was hiding when he shot the two men. Bryant had escaped the previous summer from a nearby [Lorton] prison, where he had been serving a long sentence for robbery and assault. Both agents died at the scene. Bryant was quickly captured, tried, and found guilty of the two murders, receiving a life sentence for each.

Recently married, Special Agent Palmisano and his wife Barbara had not yet moved to Washington. Palmisano's dying words were "Barbara! Barbara! I love you."

TW worked for the FBI for 28 years, during which he worked in the Cleveland, New York, and Washington, D.C., field offices and at the FBI headquarters in Washington, D.C. To distinguish himself from the many Tom Smiths who worked at the FBI, TW was identified by the initials "TW."

16. FRIENDS MADE AND LOST

"Those boys may be gone but they are not forgotten."

The experience of WW II, which Winston Churchill aptly described as "many, many months of struggle and suffering" involving "blood, toil, tears and sweat," left a lasting impression on TW and he knows he is blessed to have survived. Some of his deepest and most lasting memories, however, involve those who did not.

General Patton reminded his men in May 1945 that while "proudly contemplating our achievements, let us never forget our heroic dead whose graves mark the course of our victorious advances, nor our wounded whose sacrifices aided so much to our success." With quiet satisfaction in their accomplishments and considering the extreme circumstances experienced by the 94th Infantry Division, the many friends TW made during the war shared a common and unique bond, perhaps well beyond normal friendship. These men also are keenly aware that "all gave some, some gave all," and they often stop to remember their many friends who died on the battlefield.

TW has personally visited and photographed many of his fallen friends' graves both in Luxembourg and in the United States. Reflecting on a number of his lost friends in a March 7, 1999, letter to E-301 veteran Doug Benson, TW noted *those boys may be gone but they are not forgotten.* TW shares Patton's belief that we must "thank God that men like these have lived," and TW's sentiments are reflected in a John Maxwell Edmonds poem, which American and British troops engraved near battlefield cemeteries:

> When you go home,
> Tell them of us and say
> "For your tomorrows
> These gave their today."

Some of TW's memories of his fellow GIs, including those who were killed in action and others who have since passed away, are referenced on the following pages. Over half a century later, TW cannot help but continue to mourn these losses, despite Patton's observation that "when we mourn for such men who have died we are wrong because we should thank God that such men were born."

One of many pages in TW's scrapbook containing pictures of graves of his fellow GIs, including clockwise above Patton, Dohs, Launius, Lofblad, Platko, Thompson, Kleine, Goodlevege, Leary and Harvey.

Harry Bell Launius, Jr. *(KIA 1945, Citadel Class of 1946)*
Andrew Nourse Alexander, Jr. *(KIA, DNB 1945, Citadel Class of 1945)*

TW remembers that the Citadel contingent stayed together. On October 28, 2001, TW received a letter from Chuck Meyers, a friend that TW made at Camp Hood Texas, noting that it is a small world and explaining:

> When I read one of *The Attack* issues, lo and behold, there was Tom Smith. That name rang a bell. Could that be the Tom Smith from . . . Camp Hood? I think you were one of the Citadel guys? I was impressed.

The adjacent photo is from TW's scrapbook and is captioned "Citadel Men, Camp Hood, Texas." TW is pictured in the center, and Dave Bell is on TW's left.

TW at grave of Harry Launius, Jr., Luxembourg American Cemetry

Harry Bell Launius, Jr.

Although not graduated from the Citadel, TW attends Citadel reunions and continues to correspond with his Citadel classmates from the "War Years." Sadly, some 200 Citadel men gave their lives in WW II, and in a March 17, 1989, letter to Lieutenant Colonel Kennedy at the Citadel, TW recalled his friend and classmate Harry Bell Launius, Jr.:

> *After leaving the Citadel Harry and I ended up in the 94th Infantry Division of Patton's 3rd Army. Harry was killed in action on January 27, 1945, and is buried in the Luxembourg American Cemetery. In 1987 I visited the cemetery, paid my respects to Harry and had a photo taken of the grave.*

Harry Launius, Jr., was the only son of Harry and Sally Launius. Following his death, Harry Launius received a Bronze Star medal, a Purple Heart and a Combat Patch. His parents, Harry and Sally Launius, dedicated a WW II memorial library in Monroe, Georgia, in honor of their only son.

TW also has fond memories of a classmate named Andrew Nourse Alexander, Jr. Standing six feet, five inches tall, Andrew was an exceptional athlete at the Citadel, playing both football and basketball, in addition to being a Scholarship of Merit student.

PFC Andrew Alexander died of "battlefield disease" on August 10, 1945, in Kunming, China. After contracting malaria while serving in the signal corps, Andrew was believed to be fully recovered, but tragically died of a heart attack soon thereafter while serving food in a mess hall. After TW made a contribution to the Citadel Development Fund in

Andrew Alexander Citadel yearbook pictures

Andrew Alexander's name in 1996, TW received a letter of thanks from Andrew's only brother, Murry Alexander. In a letter to Murry dated February 20, 1997, TW recounted his memories of Andrew, noting:

> *He was head and shoulders over all of us not only in height but also scholastically and in sports ability. He used to laugh when I addressed him as "Alexander the Great."... Seeing your brother's name among those killed was an added shock. He may be gone but he is not forgotten. I am sure he is looking down on us now with smiling approval of our remembering him.*

Again in 1998, TW made a contribution to the Citadel in Andrew's name, and by letter dated January 14, 1999, Murry Alexander thanked TW again. Remembering his brother, Murry Alexander explained that "my only son is named after him," and "I always thought he was someone special, but it's unusual, I think, to have him remembered by others after so long a time." Murry Alexander passed away the following year. His son, Andrew Nourse Alexander, practices law in Mississippi.

Thomas Hopper *(Died 1960's)*

Following WW II, TW's Washington, D.C., friend Thomas Hopper attended George Washington University on the GI Bill with TW. Several years later, Hopper, whom TW describes as a very strong athlete, broke his neck while surfing at a beach on the Eastern shore. His injuries were exacerbated when the ambulance carrying him to the hospital collided with a truck. Although he had survived the perils of WW II, Hopper was paralyzed from the neck down and died several years later. During Hopper's final years, TW visited his good friend in the hospital many times, both in Washington, D.C., and later in Richmond, Virginia.

Photo of Sam D'Amico (far right) sometime before Sinz.

Salvatore "Sam" D'Amico *(Died 1980s)*

In a letter dated October 7, 1991, to Lieutenant Edmund Reuter, TW noted that in 1952 while TW was working in New York City, TW ran into Sam D'Amico, who *"had his eye shot out in Sinz."* TW recalls being very surprised when Sam called TW's name while TW was walking down the street while working in New York City. TW remembers that Sam wore a patch over his eye and understands he later received a glass eye. In TW's 1991 letter to Lieutenant Reuter, TW noted that the two men reminisced about Sinz, and that Sam D'Amico died of cancer in the 1980s.

Sinz seems to be a recurring theme in TW's written communications with his fellow veterans. Indeed, Sergeant Jack Panes of Company G, 301st Regiment once observed that when 94th Infantry Division veterans of the 301st Regiment get together, "the discussion inevitably turns to the battle of Sinz."

Merlin Vanover *(Died 1980s)*, Elwood Thompson *(KIA 1945)*

Over forty years after the war, TW met in the late 1980s with Merlin Farley Vanover (Pfc.), who served with him in the E-301 regiment and on the battlefields of Sinz. TW and Vanover were two of the six Sinz "effectives" and reminisced *"mainly about Sinz."* They then went to Arlington Cemetery to visit the grave of fellow E-301 Pfc. Elwood Thompson, who had been killed soon after the Battle of Sinz by a hand grenade.

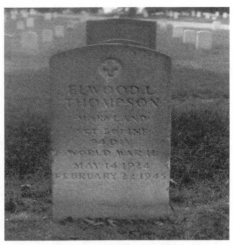

TW and Merlin Vanover at Elwood Thompson's grave at Arlington Cemetery

TW recalled a final meeting with Vanover in a December 29, 1988, letter to E-301 veteran Herb Soules:

> *A year ago he [Vanover] called me to say "goodbye." He lived in Dundalk, Maryland, and was dying from cancer. I drove over to see him the following day and he died several days later.*

Colonel Donald Hardin *(Died 1960s)*

In a December 1, 1998 letter to Lieutenant Reuter, TW remembered Colonel Hardin of the 301st Regiment, noting:

> Although he was the regimental executive officer, I saw him more overseas than I did the company commander. About 20 years ago Colonel Hardin visited Washington, D.C., and thru a mutual friend [David Bell] I arranged to have lunch with him. It was a most interesting get together.

In another letter to Lieutenant Reuter, TW noted that he and Colonel Hardin had *"reminisced again mainly about Sinz,"* and that TW had *"lost touch with Col. Hardin but in my opinion he was a fine soldier."* Colonel Hardin died a few years after TW and Bell had lunch with him.

Colonel Donald Hardin was the uncle of David Bell's wife, Pat. With only one eye, Colonel Hardin could have avoided WW II, but that was not his nature, and both TW and David Bell refer to him as *"another blood and guts."* TW noted *"it was not unusual for Colonel Hardin to come from the direction we were headed."* Colonel Hardin's son, then in his 80s, met for lunch on August 4, 2009, with TW and Janet and Dave and Pat Bell and still had the shrapnel that was removed from Colonel Hardin's leg during WW II.

Lieutenant Edmund Reuter *(Died 2007)*

Until a few years ago, TW heard every Christmas from E-301 Lieutenant Edmund Reuter. TW remembers that *"several years ago while attending a 94th Division reunion, I was told a young man was looking for me. When we connected he told me his father, Edmund Reuter, asked him to come to the reunion and look up Tom Smith. We had a nice visit, talking mainly about Sinz."*

After being wounded at Sinz, Edmund Reuter, pictured above, rejoined his Company and earned a battlefield commission of 1st Lieutenant. After WW II, he served as an infantry platoon leader in the Korean War, where he earned Bronze and Silver Star Medals. Edmund Reuter passed away from heart failure on March 4, 2007, following a career in the military. He was blessed with a long life and is survived by five sons.

Lloyd Biser *(Died 2008)*

For many years, TW and Loyd Biser of E-301 called each other on February 7th, the anniversary of Sinz. On August 25, 1987, TW met with Loyd Biser, and the two men together recalled that the six remaining "effectives" of the 1st platoon of E-301 after the Battle at Sinz included soldiers named Green, Hedrick and Lee, in addition to Farley Vanover, Loyd Biser and TW. Lloyd Biser had been a semi-professional baseball player and a resident of Rockville, Maryland. He passed away on May 27, 2008 at the age of 88 but was blessed with a long life that included six children, nine grandchildren and eleven great grandchildren. With Lloyd Biser's passing, TW is the only one of the six Sinz E-301 "effectives" still alive today.

Brad Newsom *(Died early 2000s)*

Bradford Newsom of Macon, Georgia was in Company G, 376th Regiment, 94th Infantry Division. On August 1, 1993, Newsom sent TW a letter along with the following picture. Pictured on the far right, Brad Newsom noted:

> For many years I have been trying to identify and get in touch with the person who is second from the left in the enclosed photograph. In fact, I have taken the photo to all the reunions of the 94th Division since the one in Atlanta in 1971 and showing it around asking if anyone knew who it was, all to no avail.

94th Division Soldiers, (left to right) Albert G. Harris, Jr., G-376 (Macon, Ga.), TW Smith, E-301 (Wash. D.C.), Thomas Ross Leary, E-301 (Laredo, Tx.), and Bradford Newsom, G-376 (Macon, Ga.)

After years of passing the picture around at 94th Division reunions, Brad Newsom finally received a tip from another 94th Division veteran, Frank Frauson, who was a fellow FBI agent and lunch partner of TW's and who recognized TW from the photograph. In the letter to TW, Brad Newsom explained his own experience during the war:

> In the fall of 1944 Tom Leary wrote to me and in a roundabout way to get by the censor that Marshal Leigh had been killed in the Lorient area. I received one more letter from him just before we moved to Germany. The way I heard about Leary's being killed was through Tom Buckley. I was very seriously wounded on January 17, 1945, and was evacuated to Metz, then to Bar-le-duc where I was a bed patient that the medics were trying to fly back to the USA when Tom [Buckley] came rambling through looking for people he knew and found me and told me about Tom's [Leary's] death. As I mentioned my wound was very bad. I was hit in the back left shoulder just above the armpit by a very small mortar fragment that cut the radial nerve and nicked the auxiliary artery causing an aneurysm. I was in the hospital for 17 months.

Photo taken by TW of Thomas Leary's Grave, Luxembourg American Cemetery

In a letter dated August 5, 1993, to Bradford Newsom, TW wrote:

> *Thomas Ross Leary, who is in the photo, was my best buddy. He was killed on January 20, 1945, and I was with him when he died. Tom Buckley, also a good buddy, was also badly wounded at the same time. I also knew Marshal Leigh. He was in E-301 and was among the first 94 men killed in action.*

Following their 1993 exchange of letters, TW stayed in touch with Brad Newsom and visited with him at 94th Division reunions. Brad Newson's identification of TW through an FBI agent was written up in the FBI's Grapevine magazine in January 1994 along with the picture forwarded by Brad Newsom and a headline reading "FBI at Both Ends of 'Fugitive' Hunt." Brad Newsom passed away several years ago.

Thomas Ross Leary *(KIA 1945)*

In 1974, TW learned from 94th Infantry Division veteran Richard Summers of the where-abouts of his good friend Tom Leary's grave. In a March 15, 1974, letter to Summers, TW wrote:

> I recall that Thomas R. Leary's badly torn up body was left behind when we pulled out of the woods and presumably fell into the hands of the Germans. At

the time there was some doubt as to the whereabouts of his dog tags and I had always feared that he might be classified "unknown." I am glad to learn that Tom is at rest with his buddies from the 301st.

In 1987 and again in 1994, TW visited Leary's grave in Hamm, Luxembourg.

TW still has his address book from 94th Division training camp, with many GIs names and addresses, including Tom Leary, 1616 Salinas Avenue, Laredo, Texas. Some years after the war, TW met with Tom Leary's mother and father who were visiting D.C. from their home in Texas. Tom Leary's mother passed away in 2004 at the age of 103.

Marshal Leigh *(KIA 1944)*

In a January 19, 1990, letter to Herb Soule, TW also remembered Marshal Leigh, noting:

Leigh was an ASTP buddy of mine and I, like Lew, visited his parents in Memphis. I learned that Leigh is buried in a private cemetery in St. Augustine, Fla.

Writing again about Marshal Leigh in a June 29, 1994, letter to Brad Newsom, TW wrote:

After the war Marshal Leigh's parents visited me at my house in Washington, D.C. It was a most sad affair. . . . Makes me realize how lucky we were to have survived.

Additional GIs Remembered

In a letter dated November 7, 1994, to another 94th Division veteran, TW remembered that he was *"one of eight ASTP boys assigned to E-301 and six of that group were killed in action."* TW recalls that the eighth ASTP boy was Thomas Buckley, who was wounded at Orscholz. Of the eight ASTP boys assigned to E-301 in the 94th Infantry Division, TW recalls that four of them served in TW's first platoon. In a December 1, 1998, letter to Lieutenant Reuter, TW would remember:

In March of 1944 I was one of four ASTP boys assigned to the first platoon E-301 as infantry rifleman at Camp McCain, Miss. Six months later we were in combat. You might remember them: Bernard K. Goodlevege, Samuel Harvey, Thomas R. Leary. Three of that foursome were killed in action. I am the only survivor. All are buried in the U.S. cemetery Hamm, Luxembourg. Also in that cemetery are some more boys from first platoon: Hjalmar Lofblad, Joseph Platko. In addition General Patton and our battalion commander Francis Dohs are buried there. I have learned that Morris F. Faulkner, the first boy from our platoon killed in action is in a private cemetery in Jenkinsburg, Georgia. John W. Barnes, an overseas replacement who was killed in Sinz is buried in Haverstram, N.Y. There were others whose names I do not now recall who were killed in action. Most of them were replacements.

After attending a 94th Infantry Division Association meeting in 1995, TW wrote to fellow E-301 veteran Harold Kane in August 1995 noting:

> *For me the high point of the convention was seeing you and Jim Green for the first time in fifty years. You know we went through a lot together, combat patrols, hedge rows, bullets and bitter cold.*

Harold A. Kane retired after a thirty-seven year career with the Cotton Belt Railroad in Kansas. He passed away in 2004. James W. Green retired after thirty-seven years of self-employment as a service station owner in Kentucky. He also passed away several years ago.

TW and his childhood buddies, Alan Prosise and Graham Northrup, remained very close friends long after the war and they socialized frequently. Alan Prosise died of cancer in February 1988. Graham Northrup also passed away several years ago.

17. LATER YEARS AND THOUGHTS ON THE WAR

"General Patton, I've returned, is there anything you want me to do?"

TW and Janet with son Randy at 1988 Citadel graduation.

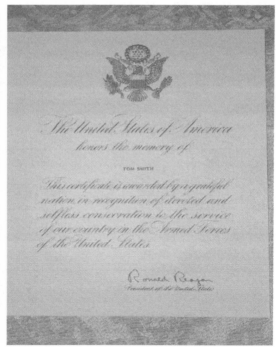

Certificate of appreciation from President Reagan

George Washington once declared that "to be prepared for war is one of the most effective means of preserving peace." TW has always believed in a strong military, and for many years, TW brought his children to the military Spirit of America performances in Washington, D.C. TW continues to maintain the utmost respect for the United States military forces, and his children report many times being told to *"Roll Out," "Forward March," "Hup, Two, Three, Four,"* or turn *"Column Left or Right."* Using two fingers from each hand, TW can whistle at a level his children believe to be louder than any other human being, which always caused them immediately to return home for dinner from the farthest reaches of the neighborhood. He also can whistle every military march song, as well as Reveille during early morning hours. Although he never graduated from the Citadel due to the intervention of World War II, one of TW's sons, Randolph Lee Smith, fulfilled TW's original goal over forty years later by graduating from the Citadel in 1988. During this same period, while TW was recognizing his son's accomplishments, President Reagan sent TW a certificate of appreciate for TW's service to his country.

TW continues to enjoy listening to WW II era music, bringing back many memories. One of TW's favorite entertainers was British singer Vera Lynn, and TW vividly remembers and still enjoys her songs, such as "We'll Meet Again," "The White Cliffs of Dover," and perhaps most of all, "Lili Marleen." Sometimes referred to as the "infantryman's anthem," Lili Marleen was written as a poem during WW I by a German Soldier named Hans Leip, who longed for his girlfriend while awaiting transport to the Russian front in 1915. Twenty-three years later, as Hitler prepared his Nazi forces to expand his empire, the poem was set to music in 1938 by German composer Norbert Schultze. "Lili Marleen" was translated into many languages and ironically was enjoyed by German, British and United States forces during WW II.

Vera Lynn's romantic and patriotic songs provided a particular inspiration to TW and the rest of the Allied troops and were often heard when troops were gathered near a radio. Many years after the war, one of TW's British friends, Bill Jones, who fought in WW II for the United Kingdom, sent TW an autographed photo of Vera Lynn (following page). The photo was accompanied by her "Compliments of Vera Lynn" stationery, on which Jones wrote:

> Once again, I must say that nothing is impossible. Dame Vera looks rather older than us—but she still sings well!

Lili Marleen

Underneath the lantern
By the barrack gate
Darling I remember
The way you used to wait
T'was there that you whispered tenderly,
That you loved me,
You'd always be,
My Lili of the Lamplight,
My own Lili Marleen

We'll Meet Again

We'll meet again
Don't know where
Don't know when
But I know we'll meet again

White Cliffs of Dover

There'll be blue birds over
The white cliffs of Dover
Tomorrow, just you wait and see.

Vera Lynn during WW II

TW's grandchildren have learned to play Lili Marleen on the saxophone and piano, and his family makes a point of singing the song at an annual Oktoberfest. In September 2009, TW was delighted to learn that Vera Lynn, at ninety-two years of age, became the oldest living artist on the British top twenty chart when her album "We'll Meet Again: The Very Best of Vera Lynn," reached the No. 20 position in England. To this day, these WW II era songs are some of TW's favorites, and a cherished memory of a difficult time.

In addition to music, TW has also enjoyed over the years an occasional entertaining remembrance of his military heritage, as noted in the pictures below. The picture at left below is of TW and Janet attending a Church Mardi Gras dance in the 1970s with TW wearing his old Citadel uniform and dressing as JEB Stuart. The 1970s picture at center is of Tom Sr., TW, Janet, and their five children dressed in Civil War era costumes, taken at an amusement park. TW's children preferred roller coasters to posing for family pictures, and they recall that the frowns on their faces were genuine. TW's son Jefferson took the picture at right in the fall of 2009 as TW was cleaning up walnuts in his backyard. Jefferson circulated the picture by email on Veteran's Day, November 11, 2009, with the caption:

> Over sixty years after World War II, Lieutenant TW Smith cannot seem to escape danger, sometimes in the most unforeseen circumstances. As I write this today, his skills are tested yet again, in a manner strangely reminiscent of his experiences against the Nazis. This time it occurs in his own back yard. A good soldier always keeps his combat gear close at hand, and Lieutenant Smith has again stepped up to the challenge. Happy Veteran's Day Dad!

TW at 94th Infantry Division Monument, Fort Benning, Ga.

TW (back row, 2nd from right) and Bill Bird (sitting, 2nd from right) with members of the Chesapeake Chapter of the 94th Infantry Division Assn.

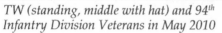

TW (standing, middle with hat) and 94th Infantry Division Veterans in May 2010

(left to right) Bob Bowden, Mrs. Bowden, Janet and TW in May 2010

Veterans Day is an important day for WW II veterans, full of speeches and decorated memorials, but more important to TW are his ongoing communications with his fellow WW II veterans. In a May 1945 memo to the Allied forces, General Dwight Eisenhower noted that "no monument of stone, no memorial of whatever magnitude could so well express our respect and veneration for their service as would perpetuation of the spirit of comradeship in which they died." TW is active in the Society of Former Special Agents of the FBI, which includes many veterans and was founded to preserve FBI friendships and loyalties and "to encourage respect for our Country, and its traditions and to foster its security and freedom from destructive forces, foreign or domestic." TW also remains active with the 301st Infantry Association and the 94th Infantry Division Association. TW still receives the FBI's *Grapevine* magazine, the 301st Infantry Association's newsletter *Hoodlum News*, and the 94th Infantry Division's newsletter, appropriately named *The Attack*. The 94th Infantry Division meets annually, albeit in decreasing numbers, and TW and his friend Bob Bowden, are the only two surviving members of E-301 who continue to attend the 94th Division Association annual meetings. TW continues to correspond with his ASTP buddy Gus Stavros, who became a successful businessman after the war and a noted philanthropist and promoter of higher education. TW makes a point of visiting graves, monuments, memorials and most importantly, WW II veterans and their families.

TW and Dave Bell in front of TW's home on June 14, 2009

One of TW's many positive attributes is his capacity for enduring friendships, which were further strengthened by WW II. Although Charlie Forrest passed away in 2008, TW and Janet continue to get together regularly with TW's high school and Citadel classmate David Bell and his wife Pat, who live in Potomac, Maryland. The two men talk frequently and attend Citadel reunions together. When asked about their longstanding friendship, Bell remarked

> I don't ever discuss with Tom my Connecticut ancestors who fought in the Union Army, including Brigadier General Edward Washburn Whitaker who served under General George Custer and carried the truce flag at Appomattox when Lee surrendered.

TW continues to wear the Citadel ring that David Bell gave him after TW lost his own Citadel ring many years ago while swimming in the Atlantic Ocean in New York. In return, TW gave Bell one of the two German iron crosses that TW had obtained during the war. On the day the photo above was taken, Bell (age 84) joked with TW (age 85) about the iron cross, asking "wasn't that the one you took from that helpless, wounded, female German soldier?" Both men continue to have vivid memories and frequently share stories of WW II and can still readily recite their serial numbers, which were issued in close sequence: TW (14192063), Dave Bell (14192130).

In 1987, TW and his wife Janet traveled to Europe and visited the American Cemetery in Hamm, Luxembourg, where many of TW's fellow GIs are buried. The couple also

TW and Janet at Luxembourg American Cemetery, 1987

visited the Lorient and St. Nazaire waterfront, where TW saw his first combat action. In addition to its WW II significance, St. Nazaire also contains a monument to the WW I soldiers who landed there during the First World War. Among these soldiers was Tom Sr.'s 42nd Rainbow Division, under the Division's Chief of Staff, General Douglas MacArthur. The site was also important to our country's founding fathers, serving as the landing point for Benjamin Franklin, who arrived there in 1776 in a desperate search for French aid during the Revolutionary War.

In October 1994, TW and his wife Janet returned to Europe with his 94th Division veteran friends for a fiftieth anniversary tour of France and Germany. The group traced the route of the 94th Division during WW II from Utah Beach through central Germany. Ceremonies were held at a number of liberated French towns, with band music and speeches by local politicians. In Pearl, Germany, a peace monument was dedicated with veterans of the German army, with coverage by CNN and the European press. TW had the opportunity to meet his German veteran counter-parts, including some from the 11th Panzer Division, and he adds in amazement *they bought us drinks.* The monument is located on the highest ridge in the area, near Sinz, and includes a letter from President George W. Bush proclaiming that "while we can never repay the fallen heroes of the 94th, we can ensure that their great deeds are not forgotten."

Like he did in 1987, TW spent hours at the American Cemetery and Memorial in Hamm, Luxembourg, locating the graves of each of his 94th division friends who were

TW (left) at Memorial Chapel, Luxembourg American Cemetery

94th Infantry Peace Monument near Sinz, Germany

killed during the war, and he took a picture of each one of them, including the graves of Francis H. Dohs, Bernard Goodlevege, Samuel T. Harvey, Harry B. Launius, Jr., Thomas R. Leary, Hjalmar L. Lofblad, Joseph P. Platko, Eugene S. Bojak, George A. Breckenridge, Michael Morris, Carl W. Nelson, and Luther L. Sellers.

During that visit, TW and his friends also took pride in visiting General Patton's grave in Luxembourg. Reverend Manning of the 301st Regiment, H Company explained during his 2008 94th Infantry Division Association memorial service in Falls Church, Virginia, that while everyone knows that General Patton received all of the credit and glory and is ranked as one of the world's greatest military commanders, "hardly anyone knows the 94th Infantry Division was Patton's strength in the capture of the Saar-Moselle Triangle and the capture of Trier. Hardly anyone knows that [94th Division GIs] were the wind beneath his wings in the race to the Rhine." Patton himself, however, did know, as reflected in his May 9, 1945, letter to the soldiers of the Third Army:

> During the course of this war I have received promotions and decorations far above and beyond my individual merit. You won them; I as your representative wear them. The one honor which is mine and mine alone is that of having commanded such an incomparable group of Americans, the record of whose fortitude, audacity, and valor will endure as long as history lasts.

Reflecting on General Patton's decision to be buried with his men in Luxembourg instead of with great military leaders at West Point or Arlington Cemetery, the Reverend Manning noted "to General Patton these bones were the bones of the best-of-the-best and the greatest-of-the-great and the reason why he chose to be buried there with his men in

Hamm military cemetery." Indeed, Patton had written previously of his desire "to lie among my soldiers" and his insistence that "in God's name don't bring my body home." Keith Shellmyer of Company A, 301st Regiment, attended Patton's rainy December 24, 1945, burial ceremony in Luxembourg, later noting, "I was very proud to have served the General in his final hour."

Quoting from General Patton's famous speech on the eve of the D-Day invasion of Normandy:

> There is one great thing that you men will all be able to say after this war is over and you are home once again. You may be thankful that twenty years from now when you are sitting by the fireplace with your grandson on your knee and he asks you what you did in the great World War II, you won't have to cough, shift him to the other knee and say, "Well, your granddaddy shoveled shit in Louisiana." No, sir, you can look him straight in the eye and say, "Son, your grand-daddy rode with the great Third Army and a son-of-a-goddamned-bitch named Georgie Patton!"

Although not quite as General Patton envisioned it, TW enjoys telling the story of how, some sixty years later, TW's three-year old grandson Garrett was sitting on TW's knee and inquired of TW's WW II experience, asking "Granddad, were you killed in the war?"

TW and Janet with grandchildren (sitting left to right): Eric Mitchell, Garrett Smith, Maddie Smith, Callie Smith, Ellie Mitchell, Connor Smith, (standing, left to right): Curtis Mitchell, Colin Mitchell, Grayson Smith

TW at grave of General Patton, Luxembourg American Cemetry

TW notes with pride that Patton's grave is marked by a simple tomb stone, the same as any other soldier's grave, and TW tells his grandchildren that while at the Luxembourg cemetery, TW circled Patton's grave and said *"General Patton, I've returned, is there anything you want me to do?"* To TW's relief, General Patton said ***nothing at all.***

In December 1994, at Fort Devens, Massachusetts, the 94th Infantry Division Association opened a historical exhibit of artifacts and memorabilia, some of which were contributed by TW. On May 8, 1995, the fiftieth anniversary of V-E Day, TW participated in the dedication of a 94th Infantry Division plaque and a "living memorial" redbud tree at Arlington Cemetery. One year earlier, TW had been appointed to a seven person committee charged with planning the memorial to the fallen comrades of the 94th Infantry Division. At the dedication ceremony, TW and his fellow 94th Infantry Division veterans listened to an opening prayer by Reverend Manning, followed by dedication remarks and Taps played by an Army bugler. The group then placed a wreath on the grave of General Harry Malony, with the General's son Jim Malony in attendance.

On Veteran's Day in 1995, TW, his wife Janet and their five children attended the site dedication for the WW II Memorial at the rainbow pool on the Mall in Washington, D.C. After President William Jefferson Clinton delivered the keynote address, a site dedication ceremony was held by scattering soil from each of the 15 American cemeteries over-

94th Infantry Division Plaque and tree dedication

TW (left) and James Blunt (L-376) next to redbud tree

Rev. Charles Manning (left) and TW (center with hat and glasses) at grave of General Harry Malony

seas where more than 93,000 WW II dead are buried and more than 55,000 missing are remembered. Included among those 15 cemeteries is the hallowed soil of the cemetery at Luxembourg, where many men of the 94th Infantry Division are buried. Sitting between the Washington Monument and the Lincoln Memorial, both of which also reflect defining moments in our nation's history involving TW's ancestors, the 7.4 acre WW II memorial site was dedicated as "a reminder of the high moral purposes and idealism that motivated the nation's call to arms as it sought victory in concert with its allies over the forces of totalitarianism."

Nine years later, the new memorial was opened to the public, and TW and his family attended the Memorial Day weekend dedication ceremony on May 29, 2004, along with 117,000 other ticketed attendees, some 60% of whom were WW II veterans and their spouses. President George W. Bush spoke, noting that "when it mattered most, an entire generation of Americans showed the finest qualities of our nation and of humanity." Other attendees included former Presidents William J. Clinton and George H.W. Bush, actor Tom Hanks, broadcaster and author Tom Brokaw, many members of congress, as well as offspring of Roosevelt, Churchill and Eisenhower. Despite many famous attend-

U.S.S. Arizona Memorial, Pearl Harbor, HI

ees, however, the focus of the dedication and memorial was on the WW II veterans, who were recognized on that day as the nation's true heroes.

In August 2005, TW received from his son Tommy a book on Pearl Harbor along with pictures of the USS Arizona and Pearl Harbor Memorial. Tommy visited Pearl Harbor on a business trip to Hawaii and took the left and right photos above of the superstructure of the USS Arizona, still visible above the water. The sunken ship remains on the bottom of Pearl Harbor, where a memorial has been constructed over the final resting place of its 1,177 crew members. The ship continues to this day steadily to leak drops of oil, which Tommy observed rising to the water's surface.

In May 2008, TW and his family, which then in-cluded eight grandchildren, attended the 94th Infantry Division Association reunion in Falls Church, Virginia. TW and Janet hosted many of the veterans at a dinner party at TW's home, during which his children pro-vided chauffeur, drink and food service and had the opportunity to meet TW's veteran friends, including the Reverend Charles H. Manning. TW continues to communicate frequently with the Rever-end Charles H. Manning (above right, during and after WW II). After serving in Company H, 301st Regiment during the war, Manning was ordained as a Baptist minister in 1953 in Millville, New Jersey. He has received awards for his moving 94th Division reunion memo-rial addresses, which he delivered year after year despite health problems.

Charles Manning was not alone in finding religion after WW II. Russ Sanoden, a 94th Division GI whose life may have been saved when TW's ASTP roommate Gus Stavros vol-unteered to escort German prisoners in his place, was fortunate to survive the war. He later entered the Lutheran Seminary and became a pastor. Regarding his decision to join the Seminary, Sanoden explained in a 1994 letter to Stavros that "there were a number of things behind my decision and I think having been in the war had something to do with it."

TW (back left) with Honor Guard, May 2010  *TW (near) carrying M-1 Garand rifle*

In May 2009, TW and Janet attended the 94th Infantry Division Association's 60th annual meeting in Nashville, Tennessee. TW was the only member of the E Company of the 301st Regiment in attendance. While reunions of the past drew over 1,000 people, the numbers have decreased over the years, while the number of veterans in walkers and wheelchairs has increased. Nevertheless, everyone was amazed to find 335 people in attendance. Despite realistic efforts underway toward "winding down our association," and a prior decision of the membership, as announced in the Winter 2009 issue of *The Attack*, that Nashville would be the final meeting, many were surprised when the members reversed themselves, voting instead for "one more meeting" in 2010.

In May 2010, TW and Janet, along with three of their children and two grandchildren, attended the 94th Infantry Division Association's 61st annual meeting in Charleston, South Carolina. TW served in the Honor Guard, carrying a model M-1 Garand rifle, which General Patton once called "the greatest battle implement ever devised." Dave Bell likewise described the M-1 Garand as a "beautiful weapon," unlike the Springfield, which "kicked like a mule." Reverend Manning was absent due to health reasons, and TW and Bob Bowden were the only attendees from E-301. Of the 94th Division's original ranks exceeding 15,000 men, 231 veterans attended the Charleston meeting, some of whom quoted General MacArthur with empathy noting that "old soldiers never die, they just fade away." With a stronger turnout than expected, the veterans voted once again for "one more meeting" in the coming year.

On August 6, 2010, the United States, for the first time ever, sent a delegation to an annual memorial ceremony commemorating the August 6, 1945, bombing of Hiroshima. The U.S. Ambassador to Japan explained that he attended the ceremony to "express respect for all victims of World War II." The ceremony, commemorating the sixty-fifth anniversary of the bombing, was held in the city of Hiroshima and included the release of 1,000 white doves as a symbol of peace. The ceremony led to renewed calls for nuclear

TW and Dave Bell (July 1943)   *TW and Dave Bell (September 2010)*

disarmament and evoked deep-rooted emotions. On August 8, 2010, TW attended a local WW II veterans' brunch at Fort Belvoir where he and fellow veterans continued steadfastly to avow that the atomic bombs saved more lives than they took.

On September 4, 2010, TW (age 87) and Dave Bell (age 86) returned to Union Station, where sixty-seven years earlier they began their long and unforgettable WW II journey. The two men reflected on their innocence and naiveté on that Summer day in 1943 when they left for Camp Lee. TW's son Tommy took their picture above in the same spot where they posed for TWs' parents, a location where little seems to have changed, but for the flags hanging for the Labor Day weekend, newer model cars, and color photographs. Once again, the two men also remembered their lost Citadel classmates, including Harry Launius, Andrew Alexander, and Jack Schnibben, and they talked about the class of 1944, which lost so many boys that it became known as "the class that wasn't."

Reflecting on WW II and TW's many friends who sacrificed their lives for their country, there were many "chance things" that may have dictated the course of TW's life or

TW presenting wreaths at Tomb of the Unknown Soldier at Arlington Cemetery, where unknown soldiers rest in "Honored Glory."

death. It might have been his bunk selection at Camp Hood when Higgins was selected as the last man for work detail; or his late night assignment to guard Lieutenant Reuter after the Lieutenant's injury at Sinz; it could have been TW's being first to pass an open window at Sinz with Hjalmar Lofblad; or perhaps his leaving the room before Elwood Thompson accidentally triggered a hand grenade; it might also have been TW's German prisoner identifying minefields at Sinz; or maybe frostbite, trench foot or even OCS. Such are the chance circumstances of war and life. But TW has always been quick to pause and remember his many friends whose chance circumstances were different.

The first page of TW's WW II scrapbook states "In Humble Gratitude to those Soldiers of the 94th Infantry Division who gave their lives for their Country." It is perhaps not surprising to TW that since 1937, spanning most of TW's life, there are U.S. soldiers who continuously honor and guard the Tomb of the Unknown Soldier at Arlington Cemetery for each minute of each day and night, year after year, while most Americans go on with their daily lives.[8] It is also perhaps not surprising to TW that for over sixty years, this assignment has proudly been carried out by the Army Infantry, specially trained soldiers of the Third United States Infantry Regiment, also known as the "Old Guard."

While TW talks about amusing WW II stories, such as the Christmas dinner story and the German prisoner in Sinz, and he jokes about what Charlie did to "make those Germans so mad," he rarely speaks of the horrific death and destruction he witnessed, and he never speaks of that which he inevitably inflicted. TW usually limits his comments about the war to amusing stories or basic facts, as opposed to feelings and emotions.

---

8   Starting in 1926, three years after TW's birth, thru 1937, the tomb was guarded during daylight hours.

More than sixty years after the war, TW's son Jefferson sent TW an email in March 2009 asking about the Movado watch that TW received as a gift from his parents and wore throughout the war, asking " was it a source of strength during the war, was it a remembrance of home?" Never one to wax sentimental, TW responded by email:

No, it was just a timekeeper. Dad

Regarding TW's father, however, his children point out that the single and only instance in their entire lives when they have ever seen tears in TW's eyes was during the funeral of his father, Tom Sr.

With selfless courage and determination, TW and his fellow veterans faced great adversity during WW II, which the Reverend Charles Manning aptly described in a 1996 address to the 94th Infantry Division Association:

> World War II was the only truly global war ever recorded in the history of mankind. God forbid there should be another. Millions of people were shot— hung—bombed—starved—gassed—frozen or drowned. It was a war in which the combatants found more ways to enslave—murder—annihilate and torture their victims than mankind has ever known.

Quoting again from Winston Churchill, however, the GIs recognized that:

> One ought never to turn one's back on a threatened danger and try to run away from it. If you do that, you will double the danger. But if you meet it promptly and without flinching, you will reduce the danger by half. Never run away from anything. Never!

TW and his fellow veterans did not flinch or run away, and instead readily accepted their assignments, including General Patton's seemingly unending orders to attack. The 94th Infantry Division's assignment was particularly dangerous, as noted by veteran Gus Stavros, I-376, in an oral history:

> We were the tip of Patton's army. We were the first most into Germany. I didn't realize it at the time.

Lieutenant Colonel George Whitman of the 376th Infantry Regiment likewise explained:

> The XX Corps was the fighting machine. . .that destroyed Germany, and our 94th Division was the spearhead of the XX Corps in the drive to the Rhine.

German Colonel Karl Thieme, who commanded Germany's 110th Grenadier Regiment of the 11th Panzer Division, felt the impact of the 94th Division spearhead and explained years later that "the 94th Division was considered to be one of the 'Elite' Divisions with which the 11th Panzer Division had to do battle."

Marilyn Ruzicka, spouse of an E-302, 94th Division veteran, observed in the Spring 2000 issue of *The Attack*, "they never whined about anything, they just went ahead and did what needed doing." Gus Stavros similarly adds "it was a war, we had a job to do." TW likewise has never complained about the cards he was dealt and the tribulations of war as a private infantry rifleman on the front lines of the Western Front. Although TW carefully picks comfortable shoes, he also has never complained about the recurring pain in his feet during cold weather over the past 60 years, nor does he complain about his continued hearing loss resulting from the war, which culminated in the recent addition of hearing aids in both ears. Despite sharing the horrors of war, TW and his fellow veterans have shown a unique ability to move on with life. Mrs. Ruzicka further aptly observed:

> The World War II veterans are really a special breed. They grew up during the Great Depression, fought in a great war, came home and bought the greatest number of houses this nation has seen, sired the "baby-boomers," saw and took part in the growth of air travel, bought cars in record numbers, sent their kids to college in record numbers, went from radios to television and right on to computers and the electronic age. They retired in record numbers and they traveled in record numbers. Indeed they were quite a generation!

TW did all of the above but does not think of himself as anything out of the ordinary, nor does he boast about anything, other than his grandchildren—Colin, Grayson, Connor, Curtis, Garrett, Ellie, Eric, Callie and Maddie.

While TW quickly moved past the war and on with life, one longstanding influence of the war may be TW's belief in the need and right to bear arms. This may be attributed to being reared during the Great Depression by a WW I veteran and working for the FBI. Perhaps TW took heed of General Patton's advice to be prepared because "you never know when some crazy sons of bitches like Hitler and Mussolini will come along and start another war." TW may also have listened to President Theodore Roosevelt's earlier advice that one should "speak softly and carry a big stick." Like his father, Tom Sr., TW has a calm and quite demeanor, but he has always possessed many guns and kept *"one on every floor of the house."* When asked about the fact that these guns are loaded, TW's sentiments are expressed by his son Randy, who explains "of course . . . it's only a hammer otherwise."

TW, then and now, still able to wear his 94th Infantry Division uniform, although noting "it was a little tight....would you believe it shrank after all these years?"

TW raised his children from a young age shooting soda cans in Alabama creeks with 38 and 45 caliber pistols and 22 caliber rifles, however, his character is much like that described of his Revolutionary War ancestor, Captain Ninian Steele:

> While he did not hesitate, as we believe, to act the soldier in war, he was emphatically a man of peace in times of peace.

Indeed, like Ninian Steele's efforts "to stop a neighborhood broil," it is not uncommon for neighbors to seek counsel from TW, and there have been multiple incidents over the years where feuding neighbors came to the house to meet separately with TW in search of resolution. Quoting again from one of the many inspirational memorial messages of Reverend Charles Manning (Company H, 301st Regiment; 94th Division):

> The God who blessed America in World War II, an unknown invisible rescue squad became a very present help in the time of trouble through a divine cause, which produced a divine effect, saving a number of lives by shortening the war.

The three words "Praise the Lord" fit perfectly, the three notes in each of the segments of Taps. When the trumpeter plays Taps, thoughtfully praise the Lord with each of the seven segments of Taps.

When Taps is finished I want you to know that on this occasion—at this time—you are "one of a kind."

Despite a common name, TW certainly is one of a kind. He would tell you that there are many thousands of WW II GIs with similar stories, and over 400,000 with the most tragic of endings. While many Americans are familiar with TW's war hero, General George Smith Patton, Jr., there are thousands of other WW II American heroes, like Edmund Reuter, James Green, and Thomas Leary, of whom most Americans have never heard and likely never will. While we Americans continue to exalt our athletes and entertainers, there are many more veterans who have fought, sacrificed, and been wounded or killed in wars during the course of American history and that live and die in relative obscurity. Many of us have unknowingly passed WW II veterans on the streets or in grocery stores, unaware of their sacrifice, heroism and accomplishment, which General Eisenhower noted "astonished the world." Fortunately, this nation's veterans are not deterred, as recognized by President Obama in a November 2010 Veteran's Day proclamation explaining that "America's sons and daughters have not watched over her shores or her citizens for public recognition, fanfare, or parades. They have preserved our way of life with unwavering patriotism and quiet courage. . . ."

Franklin Roosevelt once observed that:

There is a mysterious cycle in human events. To some generations much is given. Of other generations much is expected. This generation of Americans has a rendezvous with destiny.

There is much to be learned from this "greatest generation," and TW's family, a generation to whom "much is given," will never forget the many heroes of WW II and the U.S. military, and will continue to honor the memory of TW's fellow GIs lost in WW II. While TW was blessed with five children and nine grandchildren, he will always remember the many fallen GIs whose fate did not include the chance to raise a family. Quoting Albert Einstein:

A hundred times every day I remind myself that my inner and outer life are based on the labors of other men, living and dead, and that I must exert myself in order to give in the same measure as I have received and am still receiving.

The labors of these men are embodied in the American Flag, about which President Woodrow Wilson once explained:

The things that the flag stands for were created by the experiences of a great people. Everything that it stands for was written by their lives. The flag is the embodiment not of sentiment, but of history.

In 2007, TW attended the 58th reunion of the 94th Infantry Division in Cincinnati. During the reunion ceremonies, the Reverend Charles Manning delivered his customary memorial message, which was reported in the Summer 2007 issue of *The Attack*, to include:

> Known only by God who blessed America, on Monday, March 19, 1945, the final barrier to ending the hell on earth experience of World War II in the European theater of operation had been removed.

> Known only by God who blessed America, He had chosen the 94th Infantry Division to be the tip of the spear that pierced the brain of Adolf Hitler causing him to face reality.

> Known only by the God who blessed America, He had chosen the 94th Infantry Division to be "the straw that broke the camel's back."

TW's family will be forever grateful to TW and the 94th Infantry Division, which in the words of scripture "fought a good fight" and "kept the faith," ultimately paying extraordinary sacrifices to break the camel's back. TW's family shares the sentiments of the Division History's closing lines, expressing "hope that peace for all time may follow their travail and that the spirit that forged them into a single, invincible instrument may carry over into the peace to the power and glory of our American civilization." It is fitting that this story ends with the final poetic words of TW's 1943 centennial edition Citadel yearbook, *The Sphinx*:

> In the twilight of the years,
> When man does pause to pray,
> His heart is filled with thankfulness,
> That God's will is still man's way.

And as he prays so fervently,
God grants him courage anew,
Courage that will enable him
A greater task to do.

And when the prayer is ended,
And he no longer sees the sun,
He is humbly proud in the resolve
That God's will will be done.

SOURCES

TW Smith interviews (throughout 2009 and 2010), three and a half-page written summary of WW II memories, and many letters to and from TW and his fellow WW II veterans.

Edmund Reuter's 34-page handwritten summary of WW II memories.

David Bell interviews (June 14, 2009, June 23, 2010, September 4, 2010 and December 29, 2010)

Bob Bowden interviews (May 22, 2010 and June 1, 2010)

The Sphinx, One Hundredth Anniversary Edition of The Citadel Yearbook, 1943

History of the 94th Infantry Division, WW II, edited by Lt. Laurence Byrnes, Washington Infantry Journal Press, 1948

Blood, Sweat, and Tears, Winston S. Churchill, preface and notes by Randolph S. Churchill, 1941; and TW's Citadel Book Report of *Blood, Sweat and Tears*

On the Way: The Story of the 94th Infantry Division, published by the Stars & Stripes in Paris in 1944-1945.

Patton's Pawns, The 94th US Infantry Division at the Siegfried Line, Tony Le Tissier, 2007

Patton's Third Army, Charles M. Province, 1972

Spring and Fall 1989 Issues, and Summer 2007 Issue of *The Attack*, the 94th Infantry Division Association Newsletter

94th Infantry Division 301st Infantry Regiment WW II Historical Reviews, vol. 2, no. 3.

General Order 121, December 22, 1945, Dwight Eisenhower, Chief of Staff

Patton's Push to Trier, Nathan Prefer, World War II, February 1996

Baby It's Cold Outside, Bob Higgins

Saga of the 94th Infantry Division, 94th Infantry Division Association

Gus Stavros, Oral History, Special Collections Librarian, Poynter Library, University of South Florida, St. Petersburg, January 2009

Missing Air Crew Report, 15th AF, 461st Bomb Gp, 765th Bomb Sq.—http://www.461st.org/PDFs/MACR%209885.pdf

"War Buddies Reunited," *Anderson Independent-Mail, Sunday Magazine*, February 26, 1989

Headquarters 94th Infantry Division, Office of Chief of Staff, Resume of Important Telephone Conversation (Cedar 6, Comet 6; Major General Walton H. Walker, XX Corps, and Major General Harry J. Malony, 94th Division), February 15, 1945; February 21, 1945; March 17, 1945.

Patton's Ghost Corps, Cracking the Siegried Line, Nathan Prefer

Memoirs of a Rifle Company Commander in Patton's Third U.S. Army, Lieutenant Colonel George Philip Whitman, 1993

The Attack, vol. 51, no. 3, Spring 2000; vol. 61, Summer 2009; vol. 62, no. 1, Summer 2010

94th Infantry Division, 301st Infantry Regiment WW II Historical Reviews, vol. 2, no. 2, and vol. 2, no. 3.

94th Infantry Division Association 46th Annual Memorial Service, "America the Impossible Dream," Louisville, KY, June 3, 1995, Chaplain Charles H. Manning (H-301, 94th Division, XX Corps, Third Army)

94th Infantry Division Association 56th Annual Memorial Service, "The Eighth Wonder of the World, By the Grace of God," Milwaukee, WI., May 28, 2005, Chaplain Charles H. Manning (H-301, 94th Division, XX Corps, Third Army)

94th Infantry Division Association, 58th Annual Memorial Service, "Patton's Golden Nugget was One of a Kind," Cincinnati, OH, May 26, 2007, Chaplain Charles H. Manning (H-301, 94th Division, XX Corps, Third Army)

94th Infantry Division Association 59th Annual Memorial Service, "Patton's God Squad," Washington, D.C., May 31, 2008, Chaplain Charles H. Manning (H-301, 94th Division, XX Corps, Third Army)

The 94th Infantry Division, "The Wind Beneath the Wings of Victory," Chaplain Charles H. Manning (H-301, 94th Division, XX Corps, Third Army)

Hoodlum News, 301st Infantry Association, Summer 2009, 102nd Edition

"The 94th Infantry Division, 301st Infantry Regiment at Orscholz," Eddie Maul

SS Uniforms, Insignia, and Accoutrements, A study in photographs compiled by A. Hayes. Schiffer Military History

Captain Ninian Steele and His Descendants, Newton Chambers Steele, M.D., published by the MacGowan & Cooke Co., Chattanooga, Tenn. (1901)

The Steeles and Related Families, Katharine Anderson (1975)

The Thompson's, family history compiled by Kathleen Dement Thompson, New York City, (1905)

Confederate records of the National Archives, Washington, D.C. and the State of Alabama, Department of Archives and History, relating to Albert Henry Smith and John Green

Lincoln Legends, Myths, Hoaxes and Confabulations Associated with Our Greatest President, Edward Steers, Jr., 2007.

"Celestial Sleuth," Smithsonian Magazine, April 2009.

"Hell is Highwater" (The True Story of the WW II Cruiser the USS Indianapolis and its Crew), www.stackjones.com/sshellhighwater.html.

Truman, David McCullough, 1992

1776, David McCullough, 2005

The 94th Infantry Division Association website—http://www.94thinfdiv.com/

FBI website—http://www.fbi.gov/libref/hallhonor/palmwood.htm

Georgetown University website—http://www12.georgetown.edu/students/organizations/rotc/bnhistory.html

The Citadel website—http://www.citadel.edu/citadel-history/war-deaths/world-war-ii.html

American War and Military Operations Casualties: Lists and Statistics, Congressional Research Service Report for Congress, September 15, 2009

The Greatest Generation, Tom Brokaw, 1998

The Greatest Generation Speaks, Letters and Reflections, Tom Brokaw, 1999

The Rise and Fall of the Third Reich, A History of Nazi Germany, William L. Shirer, 1960

In Memoriam, George S. Patton, Jr., General U.S. Army, printed by 667, Engr. Reproduction Train

94th Division Association Commemorative History, 1950-1989

94th Division Association Commemorative History, volume II, 1996

A History of the English Speaking Peoples, Vol. IV, Part I, The Noblest War, Sir Winston Churchill, 1958

The Second World War, John Keegan, 1989

Patton, A Genius for War, Carlo D'Este, 1995

Patton, The Man Behind the Legend, 1885-1945, Martin Blumenson, 1985

Hitler, 1936-1945 Nemesis, Ian Kershaw, 2000

"USS Indianapolis Resurfaced, History Undercover," November 8, 2001 (126 Military History Channel)

Naval Historical Center Online Library, Department of the Navy (http://www.history.navy.mil/photos/sh-usn/usnsh-l/id1326.htm)

U.S. Holocaust Memorial Museum, Washington, D.C.

"The Hazards of War, A World War II Veteran Tells His Story, At Last," Leonard Felson, Seasons of Glastonbury, Autumn 2010

National WW I Museum at Liberty Memorial, Kansas City

The Era of J. Edgar, Joseph D. Purvis, 1997

Presidential Proclamation—Veterans Day; President Barack Obama, November 5, 2010

CREDITS

Design and layout by Scheren Communications

2010 TW family photographs taken by David Hathcox Photography

TW backyard photo edited by Vsev Horodyskyj

Made in the USA
Las Vegas, NV
02 September 2021